Amazing Grace

Watchman Nee

Christian Fellowship Publishers, Inc.
New York

Amazing Grace

Copyright © 2014
Christian Fellowship Publishers, Inc.
New York
All Rights Reserved.

ISBN 13: 978-1-937713-35-5

Available from the Publishers at:

11515 Allecingie Parkway
Richmond, Virginia 23235
www.c-f-p.com

Printed in the United States of America

Preface

"Grace and truth came [or subsists] through Jesus Christ" (John 1:17b ASV, and Darby in brackets). The Greek word for "came" is *ginomai* which means "has come"—signifying that that which before had never actually been in being in the world now begins to be so. In other words, grace actually commenced to be, yet not in God's mind, of course, but in revelation and actual existence down here on the earth (see Darby's footnote discussion on "subsists" in John 1:17). Mankind could not fully understand what divine grace is till it was revealed in Jesus Christ; nor could believing mankind fully apprehend the depth of that grace till it be found in Christ Jesus. Even today this so great salvation continually amazes those of us who have been touched by God's grace.

In August 1937 brother Watchman Nee gave a series of ten messages in Singapore on the Biblical theme of Amazing Grace. They were greatly appreciated at that time by those who heard. Now for the first time they have been translated into English for the benefit of the English-speaking world. May God use these messages to strengthen our faith.

Amazing Grace

Amazing grace—how sweet the sound—
That saved a wretch like me!
I once was lost, but now am found,
Was blind, but now I see.

'Twas grace that taught my heart to fear,
And grace my fears relieved;
How precious did that grace appear
The hour I first believed!

The Lord hath promised good to me,
His word my hope secures;
He will my shield and portion be
As long as life endures.

Through many dangers, toils and snares,
I have already come;
'Tis grace hath brought me safe thus far,
And grace will lead me home.

When we've been there ten thousand years,
Bright shining as the sun,
We've no less days to sing God's praise
Than when we'd first begun.

—John Newton

Contents

1. FORGIVENESS AND JUSTIFICATION 9
2. THE DEATH AND RESURRECTION OF CHRIST (1) .. 25
3. THE DEATH AND RESURRECTION OF CHRIST (2) .. 41
4. "RECKON" 57
5. LIVING FAITH 71
6. THE REVELATION ON THE MOUNTAIN 87
7. HOW GOD ACCOMPLISHES HIS PURPOSE (1) 105
8. HOW GOD ACCOMPLISHES HIS PURPOSE (2) 123
9. THE VICTORIOUS LIFE 141
10. THE VICTORIOUS WAY 157

Scripture quotations are from the American Standard Version of the Bible (1901), unless otherwise indicated.

1: Forgiveness and Justification

"According to law, I may almost say, all things are cleansed with blood, and apart from shedding of blood there is no remission" (Hebrews 9:22).

"Whom God set forth to be a propitiation, through faith, in His blood, to show his righteousness because of the passing over of the sins done aforetime, in the forbearance of God; for the showing, I say, of his righteousness at this present season: that he might himself be just, and the justifier of him that hath faith in Jesus" (Romans 3:25, 26).

"Who was delivered up for our trespasses, and was raised for our justification" (Romans 4:25).

THE PURPOSE OF GOD

What is God's purpose towards man? His purpose is to gain many sons (see Hebrews 2:10). You all know that for a child to be an actual son of yours he must have been born to you and not have been acquired from the outside; that is to say, your son must have your life. Only he who is born by *your* life is actually your son, whereas he who is born through others' life is not really your son. In order to gain many sons, God must cause us human beings to have His life; for only after God has given us His life can we truly be deemed His sons. This is what has been revealed to us in the Bible, and this is the purpose of God in relation to us human beings.

FORGIVENESS AND JUSTIFICATION ARE REMEDIAL

We humans, however, have sinned; and hence, God's purpose suffered a great setback. Man not only failed to receive God's life, he also fell into sin. And thus it complicated God's work and purpose. When at the beginning God created Adam, He wanted him to have a life like His. If this should become factual, God's purpose would be fulfilled. Yet Adam sinned and had now fallen, so he could not possess God's life. Accordingly, before God could ever in future give His life to man, He would first have to solve man's problem of sin. He needed to remove this hindrance of sin first and then give His life to man. God had therefore to work to resolve the fact of Adam's fall before He could obtain His purpose in man.

For this reason the Bible speaks of forgiveness and justification, which is to be the means by which God is to redeem Adam's failure. Yet let us not conclude that once man's sins are cleansed, God's purpose will have been achieved. Not so, for even should fallen man's sins be cleansed, he will merely have returned to what Adam's position had initially been in the Garden of Eden. For at that time Adam had not obtained God's life and God's purpose for him had not yet been fulfilled. Therefore, we must understand that forgiveness and justification are only the remedial process; they are actually passive in

Forgiveness and Justification

nature. Only after such a process has been concluded will we come to know what is God's purpose.

God needs to eliminate man's hindrance of sin before Him first before He could give man His life. Suppose you come to a house which you wish to enter but you find that the door is locked. Obviously your motive and aim is not to open the door but to gain entrance. Yet if the door is not opened first, your aim of entering cannot be achieved. Likewise, God's aim or purpose is for us sinners to be His sons, but first we must experience the forgiveness of our sin. Even so, that is not God's purpose but is only the removal of the hindrance to our obtaining God's life.

Hence, in our considering together God's purpose for man, we must initially look into this passive remedial process whose elements are the forgiveness of sin and justification. Most likely many of you present here have already been saved and are familiar with this subject; nevertheless, it will be helpful to review it before proceeding further.

SIN: A MATTER BEFORE GOD AND NOT JUDGED BY MAN'S CONSCIENCE

Please understand that what the Bible calls sin refers to that which is deemed to be sin against or before God, not to that which we consider to be sin before ourselves or others. In other words, the Bible's reference to sin is not a speaking of what you or I feel about what is sinful nor of what our conscience deems to be sin. On the contrary, the Bible speaks of sin as that which is done before God. In brief, what sin is, according to the Bible, is the sin before or against God. This is made clear in what David in Psalm 51 acknowledged to God: "Against thee, thee only, have I sinned, and done that which is evil in thy sight" (v. 4a). Here the words of David do not speak of sinning against man at all—neither against Uriah whom David had had murdered nor against Bathsheba, Uriah's wife—but his words only speak here of sinning against God.

It is indeed a most amazing fact that all the "sin" mentioned in the Bible is considered to have been sins committed against God; whereas we humans usually characterize those acts as sinful which from our perspective we perpetrate against other human beings— those such as arson, stealing, adultery, lying, and other such "bad" conduct. But in the Scriptures God makes clear that every sinful act is deemed to be an act of sin committed before or against Him without regard to whether such acts are good or bad in character. According to God's word, His judgment of what is sinful is not based on whether we view a given sinful act as clean or defiled or whether we deem a given sinful act as having been committed out of humility or pride; rather, the Bible declares that before God all such actions are sinful.

A month ago Shanghai had a new law requiring that all cars must park on the left side of the street. Should a

Forgiveness and Justification

car be parked on the right side, there will be a fine of five dollars. I have a friend whose store is situated on the right side of the street. For him to have to park his car on the street's left side opposite his store would be very inconvenient, given the particular street situation in the area. So, he continued to park his car at the very door of his store. Within a short time thereafter he got a ticket requesting him to appear in court three days hence.

The judge was going to demand that he pay the five-dollar fine. But my friend told the judge: "My store is situated on the street's right side; and thus, for me to park my car on the right side is most logical, I'm parking my car right before my own door. Is it therefore wrong to place my car at my very own door?" The judge replied, "Yes, you are being very reasonable, you yourself seeing nothing wrong. However, my judgment in this case before the court does not depend on you seeing nothing wrong but depends on my seeing and concluding that you are in fact wrong. And if you continue to consider that you have done no wrong and park your car at the same place, I shall fine you again." Similarly, the Bible states that wrongdoing is something God determines: it is God who decides whether you or I have sinned and not what we may say or conclude about it.

Many are confused on this subject. They insist upon maintaining that if their conscience does not bother them, that proves they have not sinned. But the issue is not determined by your conscience but by God's judgment. Even if a hundred consciences consider your or my conclusion as right, we are still being sinful. Therefore, sin is basically a matter before God, it is not a matter decided by man's conscience. An action's relation to conscience comes only after God has judged it sinful. When we realize that we have sinned before God, then our conscience becomes uneasy. Let us consider once more the case of my friend who found it convenient to park his car before his door but was fined five dollars for doing so because the judge found him to be guilty of violating the law. Do any of us think my friend would have felt safe were he to have parked his car again before his door? I can confidently answer that were he to have still parked his car outside the door of his store, the moment he would have entered his store, he would immediately have looked about to see if there were any police around; for he had by now become aware of the law, and his conscience would hence feel uneasy.

    Before we see God we do not know what sin is or feel sinful. Not until one day God opens our eyes to see what He has seen does our conscience begin to feel uneasy. In order to save us, God must do two things. The first is to rid us of our sins before Him. The second is to place His life in us. Before we can receive God's life, we must first be rid of the sins that stand against the life of God.

Forgiveness and Justification

Forgiveness of Sin Based on God's Righteousness

How does God get rid of man's sin before Him? It is through the shed blood of the Lord Jesus. God sent to the world His Son, clothed with a human body, who then died on a cross, shedding His blood to redeem us of our sins before God. It is through the blood of Jesus that our sins before God are forgiven and our conscience is pacified (see Hebrews 9:14).

I once traveled with a friend to Jiujiang. On the way we met a Muslim missionary. My friend asked him what was the hope of his faith. He answered that if a person repented of his sins, Allah would forgive him and cause him to go to heaven. My friend further asked that if that person sinned again after repentance, then what would be the outcome: where had his sins gone after being repented of? He replied that Allah was not so particular, that Allah would be flexible if he saw true repentance. So my friend said to the Muslim missionary that his god was too careless, that only the Christian God was righteous.

We should realize that to repent is one thing and the effect of sin is another. For instance, suppose I beat Mr. Tang tonight so severely that his body is full of bruises but tomorrow I repent and feel regretful. Is the matter solved? No, Mr. Tang's body will still be in a severely bruised state. The effect will still be there, and nothing is resolved. Or, if you borrow a thousand dollars from a friend, will the matter be cleared up later just by your repentance for not having paid the loan back? No, for repentance is one thing, but the unpaid debt is still there. Such is the way God forgives our sins: He cannot forgive our sins carelessly: He first needs to punish sin before the matter can be resolved.

Again, suppose a person who has robbed is arrested by the governor. Due to the fact that this arrested person has at home an eighty-year-old mother and a three-year-old child, the governor shows pity on him and releases him. Should this governor continue to show such mercy, he will eventually be dismissed from his office for the district shall otherwise be full of robbers. If there is lawlessness in the land, the governor must treat such according to law. Else if he releases the lawless one, he will himself be deemed to be acting unlawfully.

For God to be able to forgive our sins, He must maintain righteousness. I know a friend whose father was a city mayor. He had been so for several years. There were many bandits in that place. And it turned out that he had used certain public funds—funds which had been designated to be used for other purposes—with which to capture these bandits. Although he spent tens of thousands of the public's predesignated money, he had not embezzled any of it. He had wisely used the money for the purpose of apprehending the bandits. Not long ago the district government arrested the mayor and was going to punish him by sentence of death, for the law held that any public servant who misuses designated public funds must be shot. This mayor happened to be my fellow worker's father and my fellow worker was

Forgiveness and Justification

understandably highly agitated. Since I knew some high officials in the government, I wrote letters to them and later visited them personally in an attempt to convince them that the public funds had not been taken by him to his home for his own use. But they told me: "Mr. Nee, we know the whole story. We also want to help, but we can find no way through. True, we have the authority to release him; but if we do, how can we be complying with the law? Unless we can find a way that will satisfy the law, we will be lawless if we release him."

God wants to forgive our sins, but He will not compromise himself. He orders us to keep the law, for He himself always does so. He told Adam: "In the day that thou eatest thereof thou shalt surely die" (Genesis 2:17). If, when Adam and Eve had disobeyed and eaten the fruit of the tree of the knowledge of good and evil, God had not put them to death, He himself would have been considered to be a liar. We do not know what righteousness is, or what is the law. But for God to forgive our sins and save us, He must adhere to His character, His righteousness, and His law. He cannot free us and himself behave unrighteously. He cannot save us and create a problem for himself.

A year ago in Shanghai there was a sister in the Lord who was superintendent of nurses in a hospital. She was also responsible for the management of all the medicines there. One day another Christian sister came to me to speak to me about her. I said that this nurse was a very good sister, but this other sister strongly responded that it was not so. I also said that the nurse loved the Lord and had also witnessed for Him in the hospital, so she was very good. Yet this other sister responded by saying that the nurse could not be considered to be a good sister if she did not even know what righteousness was. "The other day," she reported, "my child was sick. I did not have the money to see a doctor. So I brought my child to her. She was most willing to help by applying medicine on the wound and binding the wound with cotton. When I asked for the cost, she refused to tell me, she saying that the hospital had lots of medicine. I could do nothing more, so I returned home. Though she had helped me, I felt uneasy about the incident since the medicine and cotton had belonged to the hospital. She should not have stolen the medical supplies belonging to the hospital in order to help me."

Similarly, God could not have saved us without making rightful compensation. Otherwise, we would say, How can a righteous God save us unlawfully? A policeman cannot apprehend a lawless person and then turn around and set him free. We who have sinned need to be judged and punished. Should God fail to punish us He will be unrighteous.

So what should be done? Suppose Mr. Tang is a rich person. I borrow ten thousand dollars from him and promise to pay it back in twenty years. But after twenty years I go to Mr. Tang and state: "I am now very poor and unable to repay you. Will you please have pity on me, forgive my debt, and give back to me the I.O.U. note?" He will reply that it had been agreed that I would pay him back in twenty years. "Indeed," says Mr. Tang, "your agreement is right here. You have signed, and so have I. And now twenty years have passed. If you don't pay me back, we will have to solve the matter according to the law." But I would say, "Please have mercy on me for I have no way to pay you back. Will you please give me back the I.O.U. note?" What do we think about this? Please bear in mind that if I do not pay the loan back, I shall be breaking the agreement; and if Mr. Tang does not demand that I repay, he too will be breaking the contract. A debt that is not resolved properly by both parties will cause both the borrower and the lender to be lawless persons. The only difference between these two individuals is that one violates the law badly while the other one does so honorably.

The Lord Jesus Shed His Blood to Clear Away Our Debt of Sins

What way does God use to forgive our sins as well as preserve His integrity? It is easier to simply forgive, but to forgive righteously and lawfully is difficult. Let me use the illustration again of the wealthy Mr. Tang. And let us suppose that he has much more than the ten thousand dollars he lent me twenty years ago and which I was unable to pay back, thus violating the agreement we both had signed. One day he comes to my house. In the beginning his words are rather harsh. At first he says that a contract cannot be changed, so I must pay him back the money I had borrowed from him. But then he softly speaks these words: "Here are ten thousand dollars which I want to give you as a gift, whereas the money I formerly lent you was borrowed according to the contract we both had established back then. Now, though, this ten thousand is freely given to you." Without saying any more, he leaves. And suppose further that the next morning I take the money Mr. Tang had given me yesterday and go to his home with confidence and say to him that this is the money I owe him. And in response he says, "Fine," and gives me back the I.O.U. note. This can illustrate for us the law of God and God's interaction with it.

God has said to man, "Keep My law and live, or else you shall certainly die." If we violate His law, God will not offer to save us from this sentence of death carelessly. Once having given us His law, God himself cannot violate it. What, then, does He do to save us? God gives us His beloved Son. God's means of rescuing us from death is not a matter of law but is beyond law. It is out of God's love that He gives His only begotten Son to us, for Him to shed His blood for us and pay back all our debt of sin to God. And thus, through the Lord Jesus' blood, we can with confidence draw near to God. Such is the means God uses to save us. So that all who are now in Christ Jesus have their sin debt already paid back. Moreover, God will never ask us for any further payment because

Forgiveness and Justification

our sins were not forgiven easily or carelessly but rather were righteously judged at Calvary; and hence, we received the proof of sins' forgiveness through Christ Jesus. This is just like the story of me with Mr. Tang: I repaid my debt to Mr. Tang who would have been unrighteous had he refused to give me back the I.O.U. note. The Lord Jesus has already cleared our sin debt, so today we can approach God with confidence. Through the blood of Christ God has saved us and this salvation has fully satisfied God's righteous demand. Please therefore remember that the evidence of sins forgiven is God's righteousness (see I John 1:9).

Let us also bear in mind that our sins are not cheaply forgiven but that a costly redemptive price has been paid. We are saved through the shed blood of the Lord Jesus (see I John 1:7). So we now can approach God with a conscience void of offense (Acts 24:16), for the Lord has already cleansed it for us (Hebrews 9:14), and concerning which God will never make any further demand upon us. Henceforth we may offer up praises to God.

Finally, let me relate a story which I always love to tell. In 1925 I was in Nanking speaking in a girls' school. One day I was speaking on the righteousness of God. As I spoke to those girls, I sensed that they did not appear to understand. I should note, incidentally, that resting on the pulpit there was a flower pot and that the school principal was seated nearby. So I asked her, "Suppose a student breaks this flower vase. What will you do?" "Ask her to pay for it," said the principal. "What if she does not have the money?" I asked. She replied: "According to the school regulation one must pay, whether a person has the money or not." I further asked the principal this: "Suppose this is a student you love dearly and she is the smallest as well as the poorest. She has absolutely no way to pay for the broken vase. What, then, will you do?" She replied, "Now that is altogether another matter." Why could she not simply forgive the girl? The principal realized that if she did, within a few days all the other vases in the school would be broken. What should the principal therefore do? She said, "I would pay for her."

This, I said to the students, is God's reaction towards us who have violated His law. He loves us, and this love is without end. We have sinned and have no way to comply with the righteous demand of the law of God. Due, however, to His love for us, He himself came to solve our problem. He gave His only begotten Son to us as His means of paying our debt of sin for us. When I explained God's righteousness in this way, the students at the girls' school came to understand.

The next day was my last for speaking. When I entered the hall, I did not see the flower vase. I asked the principal what had happened. She answered that it had been broken. I asked if she had demanded payment. She replied that she had. So I said, "Your word has the flavor of Mount Sinai." Once in the past God had spoken

Forgiveness and Justification

in this manner, but now through the blood of the Lord Jesus our sins may be forgiven.

Suppose I had broken some law in my community and was arrested by the police. And suppose a court judge condemned me to five years of imprisonment. And suppose further that five years later I was released and I happened to meet the very policeman who had arrested me. I could now joke around with him because today he had no authority to arrest me again for the earlier crime. For my guilt had been punished and the case was forever closed. Similarly, let us praise God that in Christ all our sin debt has been paid. Such, then, is the way of God's righteous forgiveness of sins.*

---

* Note: Message given on 3 August 1937.

2: The Death and Resurrection of Christ (1)

"Who [Jesus] was delivered up for our trespasses, and was raised for our justification" (Romans 4:25).

"According to the law, I may almost say, all things are cleansed with blood, and apart from shedding of blood there is no remission" (Hebrews 9:22).

"The life of the flesh is in the blood; and I have given it to you upon the altar to make atonement for your souls: for it is the blood that maketh atonement by reason of the life" (Leviticus 17:11).

"The blood shall be to you for a token upon the houses where ye are: and when I see the blood, I will pass over you, and there shall no plague be upon you to destroy you, when I smite the land of Egypt" (Exodus 12:13).

"Inasmuch as he hath appointed a day in which he will judge the world in righteousness by the man whom he hath ordained; whereof he hath given assurance unto all men, in that he hath raised him from the dead" (Acts 17:31).

The Two Sides of God's Work

We have already seen what is the reason for the work of God. We know that God's original purpose is for man to possess His life. Unfortunately, man failed and that has complicated God's work. For today God must solve the problem of redeeming men as well as giving men His life.

Therefore, God's work towards us is twofold: to redeem us on the one hand and to arrive at His purpose in us on the other. To redeem is to solve the sin problem of men, to arrive at His purpose is to give God's life to men. In studying the Bible we come to know that this double work of God is achieved through the death and resurrection of Christ. The Lord Jesus had said that other than the sign of Jonah there would be no other given (see Matthew 12:39, 16:4). The sign of Jonah bespeaks death and resurrection. What is meant by a sign? It is that which pertains to God's work. Apart from the sign of death and resurrection God gives no other; for His work is centered on none other than death and resurrection.

There are four aspects to the death and resurrection of Christ: two of them are negative in character and the other two are positive. The two negatives deal with sin whereas the two positives deal with life-giving. It is through the realities of these four aspects of death and resurrection that we are saved and arrive at God's purpose for us. Hopefully we shall come to understand these four aspects during these conference days together.

CHRIST'S DEATH AND RESURRECTION: FOUR ASPECTS

The four aspects of the death and resurrection of Christ are these: first, the substitutionary character of

The Death and Resurrection of Christ (1)

His death and resurrection; second, our co-death and co-resurrection with Christ in His death and resurrection; third, the release of His death and resurrection; and fourth, the resistance (that is, the self-denial) of His death and resurrection. We can discern these four aspects in the Scriptures. Unless we clearly see these four aspects of Christ's death and resurrection, we shall end up in confusion concerning our labor for the Lord.

Whereas substitution and co-death/co-resurrection are for the purpose of dealing with sin, release and resistance (or self-denial) are for the purpose of dealing with life. Substitution and co-death/co-resurrection are negative in nature, but release and self-denial are positive; yet all four are for the sake of arriving at the purpose of God. At present, we will consider only the death side of these four aspects of substitution, co-death/co-resurrection, release, and self-denial. Later on, we will discuss the resurrection or life side of these four aspects. I hope you will not be concerned if at first you cannot understand these four aspects of Christ's death and resurrection. Gradually you will come to see them without any confusion.

Now we learn from Scripture that the first facet of death is the blood, the second facet is crucifixion, the third is the flesh, and the fourth is the taking up of the cross. The Holy Scriptures show us the blood, the crucifixion, the flesh, and cross-bearing; and these are the four different facets to the death of Christ.

Blood: Rids Man of Sin before God

This evening we will consider the blood and therefore, also the substitutionary character of Christ's death and resurrection. But before we do so, let us first be clear concerning the problem of sin. We have already discussed how sin is a problem to be solved before God. We also are aware that sin carries with it the matter of guilt in man. What is guilt? Well, whenever I sin I become guilty before God. It is I who commit sin, but as soon as I sin, I am a guilty person before God. So how will God deal with this situation? Before God can forgive sin He must first judge it. Only after sin has been judged can it be resolved or eliminated. For instance, if I violate the law in some way on the road, the police will apprehend me and bring me before a judge. The judge cannot simply release me. On the contrary, depending on the particular infraction of the law, I must either pay a fine or be imprisoned for a period of time before I can ever be set free.

Similarly, when we sin against divine law, God cannot immediately set us free. He must first judge our sin according to His righteousness. Yet fallen man himself is unable to satisfy God's righteous demand. So God in His great love paid sin's penalty for man. Whatever the penalty man must pay for his sin, God himself pays for it. Hence, redemption is God himself in Christ being judged and paying the sin debt for us. All is done out of God's love and depends on the blood of Christ. What is the use of Christ's blood? It is to redeem us from the penalty or wages of our sin and to satisfy God's righteous or legal requirements.

CHRIST'S BLOOD WASHES THE CONSCIENCE, NOT THE HEART

Many Christians misunderstand, they thinking that the Lord's blood is for cleansing our hearts. Blood is mentioned in both the Old and New Testaments more than four hundred times, yet it never once says that blood cleanses the heart. Christians may say so but the Bible never does. Are you surprised at this? Someone may observe: "Does not Hebrews 9:14 declare that the blood of Christ cleanses our hearts?" However, according to the Greek original, this passage does not speak of a cleansing of the heart but of the *conscience* (cf. ASV). From this and other places in the Scriptures we learn that the blood of Christ cleanses our conscience, not our heart. Why is this so? It is because the heart of man represents his very self—his real self; and this real I in man, having come from fallen Adam, is unclean in nature and can never be cleansed but must be eliminated.

The Bible describes this heart of man as stony (see Ezekiel 11:19, 36:26). How can a *stony* heart ever be cleansed? It cannot. What, then, can be done? God says in this same Ezekiel passage that this stony heart must be taken away and replaced with a fleshy heart. From this we can conclude that regeneration is not a matter of cleansing the old man but is instead a matter of getting rid of him. How can anyone wash clean a man of clay? The more a person washes such a man the dirtier he becomes. Just so is our heart situation. Hence, the Bible never mentions that Christ's blood washes the heart but says that it washes or cleanses our conscience.

What is conscience? It is that faculty in us which makes us feel either uneasy or peaceful. And what—in this context—does the Scripture mean by declaring that the Lord's blood cleanses our conscience? It means that Christ's blood removes our sins before God, for the Lord Jesus has borne our punishment before Him and our sins are being forgiven by God due to His blood. As we believe in the Lord Jesus, we know our sins have been forgiven because His blood has washed away the guilt from our conscience and given it peace. And since the conscience has now been cleansed, it no longer feels sinful.

But please note that all this is objective, it all having to do with God and nothing to do with man. Man has no need of blood; rather, blood is required by God and is the righteous demand of God. That is why Exodus 12:13 tells us that as God himself would see the blood, He would immediately pass over and spare the homes of the Israelites. And thus the focus of this Bible passage is not man seeing the blood but God doing so.

Please bear in mind that blood has nothing to do with man. Blood is to bear the righteous judgment before

The Death and Resurrection of Christ (1)

God. For without sins being judged God's purpose cannot be reached. Man having sinned, he cannot be saved except by God. From man's perspective, therefore, blood is almost totally objective. It is primarily concerned with God's side. For man blood only provides a peaceful conscience: the shed blood of God's Son removes man's guilt before God and blots out his sins before Him. The rest of what God purposes in redeeming man is to be accomplished by the other aspects of the work of the cross. So when the Bible speaks of the blood, it is first and foremost a pointing to God and His satisfaction.

THE LORD'S BLOOD ALONE IS DRINKABLE

When I was in Manila, a knowledgeable sister in the Lord inquired of me, saying: "No blood was allowed to be drunk during the age of the flood, neither was it permitted in the age of the law. Even during the time of the New Testament apostles, blood was still forbidden to be drunk. Why was it so?" I explained to her that we know that in the Bible there are altogether four ages. The ages of the fathers and of the law have already passed. Today is the age of the apostles of grace, and that of the kingdom is yet to come. During the age of the fathers God had told Noah not to drink blood (Genesis 9:4); and in the age of the law God had also said to Moses not to do so (Leviticus 17:10-12). Furthermore, in relation to the age of the apostles God has given the same instruction of not drinking blood (Acts 15:20). So I asked this sister if she had ever drunk blood. "Since the Bible says not to do so, I have never drunk any blood," she replied. I said to her, "If that is the case, then I dare not break bread with you at the Lord's Table because you are not saved but are condemned to the lake of fire." She interrupted me and responded with, "Really? I have never drunk any blood." So I said to her that I had drunk blood, and then proceeded to explain to her how and why I had done so. And upon hearing the explanation, she now acknowledged that she too had drunk blood.

Yes, the Bible does in fact tell us not to drink blood. Nevertheless, Christ's blood is truly drinkable (John 6:55). It is God's intention that we are only to drink one kind of blood. In heaven and on earth, there is this one kind of blood that is alone drinkable—thus signifying that in heaven and on earth there is but one solution to man's sin problem. Only one Savior—and thus only one kind of blood—can redeem us before God. If man refuses *this* blood, there is no more sin offering (Hebrews 10:26). Apart from this Savior and His blood there is no other way of salvation for mankind (Acts 4:12).

Thank God, this blood we have drunk. The reason the Bible forbids us to drink all other blood is for the purpose of summoning us to drink this one blood alone. Please therefore bear in mind that when the Bible mentions blood, such speaks directly or indirectly concerning the demand of God's righteousness. The blood of Jesus

The Death and Resurrection of Christ (1)

alone can redeem us of our sin and accomplish God's redemptive purpose. Through the blood of Jesus, man's sins before God are eliminated.

THE LORD'S RESURRECTION IS FOR OUR JUSTIFICATION

We know that God the Father causes His Son to shed blood in order that He could righteously forgive our sins. How do we know that the blood of Jesus is able to wash away sin? Over two thousand years ago Jesus Christ bore our sins and died on Calvary's cross. How do we know that God considers this blood as sufficient, that our sins have been wiped away, and that all this is trustworthy? Suppose God were to say Christ's blood is not efficacious, then what could we do? But we know that this blood satisfies God's requirement. This blood shed by His Son is His righteous judgment upon man's sin. He himself caused the Lord Jesus to shed blood. Yet how can we know that this judgment is sufficient, that Christ's blood has satisfied God's righteous demands? Thank God, He not only caused Christ to die, He also caused Christ to be risen from death. Resurrection is God's response as to the efficacy of the shed blood of Christ. The blood has been offered up to God, and He responded with resurrection as proof of His satisfaction. The blood has been sent from man—even the Man of God—to God, and resurrection is sent from God to man upon His having accepted the blood.

"If I be lifted up from the earth" (John 12:32a). So said the Lord Jesus. For whom and for what was He lifted up on Calvary's cross? He was lifted up to God for us and for our sins. God looked upon His death as sufficient; therefore, He caused Christ Jesus to be risen from death as His way of giving assurance to all men (Acts 17:31). The Bible has not so much called people to believe in the *death* of Christ as it has called them to believe especially in His resurrection. If we read the Bible sufficient enough times, we will be clear about this. When we persuade people to believe in the Lord, we too often call them to believe primarily in the Lord's death and thus to be saved through the Lord's blood. But where can we find in the Bible a calling of people to believe in the Lord's death and in His shedding of blood as the way to become their Savior? Let me say that many messages being given by preachers today are without scriptural basis on this point. But I would add that I request that you not tell others that Mr. Nee has stated that people ought not believe in the Lord's death or believe that the Lord's blood can redeem them of their sin; for what I have meant to say here is that when certain Bible passages are used to persuade people to believe in the Lord, these passages do not ask them to especially believe in the Lord's death but primarily call them to believe in the Lord's resurrection (see, e.g., Romans 10:9). By believing in the Lord's resurrection we are being justified (Romans 4:25)—that is to say, that God now deems us to be "just as if" we had never sinned. Hence, when the Bible calls people to believe in the Lord, it is not only a call to believe in Jesus' death but even more so a call to believe in His resurrection.

Perhaps all this will confuse you. But simply remember that the blood has its meaning and place primarily before God. Whether it can redeem man of his sin or not, let God make the determination, for Christ's blood does not primarily concern us. Since God looks upon the shed blood of Christ as sufficient to wipe away man's sin, He raises Christ from death. Accordingly, when *we* look at the blood of Christ, we are assured that the Lord's blood is dependable in wiping away our sins and causing us to be justified before God (see again Romans 4:25). The essence of this Romans 4 verse in the Greek original betokens a balance, as expressed by means of a set of opposites: on the one hand, Jesus' death is for the forgiveness and thus the elimination of our transgressions, but on the other hand, His resurrection is for our justification.

Christ's Resurrection: the Evidence of Our Justification

Now I would like to test our understanding: Was Jesus delivered up to death first or did we sin first? I believe we all know that Jesus was delivered up because men had sinned first. That being the case, then the following sequence will be true as well. We learn from Romans 4:25 that the resurrection of Jesus is for our justification;

and hence, it is because we have been justified that Christ was risen from death. Thus, the Lord's resurrection proves that we have *already* been justified before God. The proof of sins forgiven is the Lord's shed blood, and the evidence of our justification is the Lord's resurrection.

For example, I owe Mr. Tang a certain debt that is still unpaid, and so he takes me to court. The judge condemns me and sentences me to three months' imprisonment. I have no means to repay my debt. Mr. Tang is my best friend, and he also has the means to pay my debt, but instead he offers to go to jail for me. The moment Mr. Tang is imprisoned I am freed. Yet, though my body is freed, my heart is not at peace because I still wonder if my case before the court has been entirely concluded. As long as Mr. Tang remains in prison my heart has no rest. When will my heart feel peaceful? It will only happen at the moment of Mr. Tang's release from prison. Not till then is my case closed and my heart set free. In other words, Mr. Tang's release proves that my case has been totally and satisfactorily concluded. Otherwise, the judge could not and would not have set him free from prison.

At the moment of Jesus' death is the very moment that the problem of our sins is solved. But suppose up till today He has not been risen from death; would we not still wonder whether or not Christ's blood has satisfied God's righteous demand? Hence, that is why the Bible teaches that the Lord Jesus' death is especially for God

The Death and Resurrection of Christ (1)

and His resurrection is especially for us. God realizes that if we only believe in the death of the Lord, our hearts will not be at peace. Consequently, He caused the Lord not only to die but also to be raised from among the dead. So that when we see that He has risen, it proves to us that our sin case has been solved; otherwise, how could God have released Him from death's prison? Therefore, God's causing Christ to be risen from among the dead provides the evidence to us that His judgment against man's sin has been concluded. The resurrection of Christ proves that Jesus' blood has satisfied God's righteous demand.

God accepts the death of Christ, and we accept the resurrection of Christ. Hence, God has not called people to believe in Christ's death; rather, He calls us to believe preeminently in Christ's resurrection. For the resurrection of Christ proves that His death is sufficient for God and by His resurrection we are justified. So Paul wrote in Romans that Jesus was delivered up for our trespasses and was raised for our justification. In order to demonstrate that we have been justified, Jesus must be resurrected. Jesus as man went to God to pay our debt, offered up His blood to God, and was judged by God in our stead.

Suppose I owe a brother money but I am unable to repay him immediately for I do not have sufficient funds. What should I do? I will slowly accumulate money: I will gather together some money from Shanghai, from Swatow, from Foochow, from England, the United

States, the Philippines and from other places. I eventually figure that this total of funds should be enough, so I take it to Mr. Tang. I give him the money, saying to him that I have calculated that the funds given him should be sufficient to have now fully repaid him the loan. So here I would ask: Who is the one to be concerned as to whether or not the money paid back is sufficient—I or the one who receives the money? Obviously it is the one who receives the money. He is the one who must ascertain whether or not these funds gathered from hither and you are in fact usable to him and that the amount is sufficient as total repayment. On the other hand, I myself care for nothing except to receive a receipt from him indicating total repayment of the loan.

Similarly, whether the blood of Jesus is sufficient to redeem us of our sins is not a matter for us to determine; that is God's concern; He himself will see to that. Whereas the Lord's blood is for wiping away our sins before God and making repayment of our debt to Him, the Lord's resurrection—as it were—is a repayment receipt which God gives to men. Hence, Acts 17:31 declares that Christ's resurrection serves both as God's assurance to men that the blood of the Lord Jesus has eliminated their sin and as His receipt to men indicating full repayment.

What, then, do we believe when we believe in the Lord Jesus? We believe that God has raised Him from among the dead. If you should ever wonder about your

The Death and Resurrection of Christ (1)

salvation, just look at the repayment receipt God has given you. Suppose God should say that you are yet to be justified; you can simply show Him "the receipt of resurrection." You can boldly say to God: "If I am not justified, how is it that You gave me this resurrection receipt?" We know the Lord is risen and we have believed in His resurrection; therefore, we are saved.

This, then, has been a presentation of the two sides of the Lord's death and resurrection and also of the two aspects of substitution. These two aspects are objective in nature. Basically, they have nothing to do with us, since they have to do entirely with solving the problem of our sins before God. Whether or not we have been forgiven and justified, such concerns belong to God alone. May God bless us.[*]

---

[*] Note: Message given on 4 August 1937.

3: The Death and Resurrection of Christ (2)

"So now it is no more I that do it, but sin which dwelleth in me.... But if I would not, that I do, it is no more I that do it, but sin which dwelleth in me" (Romans 7:17, 20).

"Knowing this, that our old man was crucified with him [Christ], that the body of sin might be done away, that so we should no longer be in bondage to sin ... Even so reckon ye also yourselves to be dead unto sin, but alive unto God in Christ Jesus" (Romans 6:6, 11).

We have already mentioned the four facets to the death of Christ: first the blood—that He has died for us so that we may not die and that this is for the remission of our sins; second, crucifixion is for dealing with "the old man"; third, the flesh—that He was crucified so that we might receive life and that through death life is released; and fourth, bearing the cross is for dealing with the self. To put it another way, we can say that blood is for the sake of forgiving man's sins; crucifixion is for dealing with the sin nature; flesh is to cause men to have life; and cross-bearing is for dealing with the self. Hence, these various facets to the death of Christ are for giving man full salvation. Last evening we came to understand how the blood of Jesus remits or pardons man of his sins before God. This evening we will come to understand how the cross deals with the sin nature—that is to say, with the sin which dwells in us.

THE SIN BEFORE GOD AND THE SIN IN MAN

The Bible shows us two kinds of sins: one kind is that which is before God and which in the Bible's original Greek text is cast in the plural number; the other kind is that which is within us, and this kind of sin is cast in the singular number both in the Bible's English versions and in the original Greek text. Before God are the many sins which we have committed and all of which can be numbered. On the other hand, the sin within us is that kind which forces us to commit sins, to do many sinful acts. We must know the difference between the sins before God and the sin in us. "Against thee, thee only, O God, have I sinned," said David (see Psalm 51:4a). This is the kind of sin which is before God. But we also find in the Bible this: "sin which dwelleth in me," wrote Paul (Romans 7:20b). The sin here is of another kind. Thus we see that the Bible speaks of two kinds of sin; and hence, we shall see that the ways of deliverance are also of two kinds. Whereas the sins before God are to be remitted by the blood, the problem of the sin within us is to be resolved by means of another way of deliverance.

Now, then, let us see how the sin before God is different from the sin in man. Suppose a child did not like to go to bed early. He usually played till ten o'clock. At first his parents said nothing; but as his body got weaker, his parents ordered him to go to his room at eight o'clock. That evening he was not able to play outside, but was forced to enter his room. However,

The Death and Resurrection of Christ (2)

after he closed the door the boy played till ten. Initially his parents had not ordered him to go to sleep. So if he did not lay down to sleep, he had not committed any sin before his parents. If, though, one day his parents did order him to sleep but he failed to do so, then he would be committing the sin of rebellion. Such a sin would have originated from his dislike in his heart to go to sleep early. Now let us suppose that henceforth the child always closed his room door at 8 o'clock but resumed playing till ten. And suppose that at first his parents were unaware of it and that upon noticing that the child remained weak they decided to watch through a window from outside and found the child not sleeping but playing. The next morning, therefore, they scolded him. He acknowledged his sin and received forgiveness. By confessing his sin, he obtained forgiveness; but had his heart changed to his now liking to go to sleep early? Let me tell you that after eight o'clock, he would be in bed sighing for he still did not like to go to sleep early.

Please be advised that sin forgiven does not change a person to be good and not sin anymore. It is not unlike a proud person who well knows that pride is a sin and receives forgiveness through confession but who after being forgiven will not immediately become a humble person. It is also not unlike a person who has the habit of owing debt, always borrowing and borrowing till he owes ten thousands of dollars. And were he to have a good friend who would pay back for him all his past debts, would this debtor be changed to be a person not borrowing anymore? Let me tell you, his old lust shall return and he will borrow again as before. Even though our outward sins may be forgiven, the inward sin in us still needs to be dealt with.

Nowadays losing one's temper is a common failure of many Christians. When a Christian has lost his temper, he knows he was wrong and therefore asks God's forgiveness. But will he henceforth become a patient person? Let me tell you, even after he has tried to be patient once, twice and three times, his bad temper will still come back out. Therefore, even if all the outward sins are forgiven because of the Lord's blood, the inward sin remains a problem. It still needs to be dealt with. If this issue is not dealt with, and though you may be saved and born again, you are no stronger than the people of the world. Unbelievers lose their temper, but so do you. Unbelievers do wrong, but so do you. Unbelievers are proud, but you too are proud. There is no difference between you and the world.

Man's Inward Sin: a Law

What is inward sin? Inward sin is a law of the flesh (Romans 7:23, 25b). What is law? A law is that which happens always and forever the same. For example, a law of the country says that he who kills must pay with his life, that whoever kills must himself be killed: if you kill this year, you will pay with your life, and if you kill next year, you must still lose your life. This law being

The Death and Resurrection of Christ (2)

passed will never change so long as such law remains in effect. Likewise, gravitation is a law—in this case a law of nature. If you drop an object, it immediately falls down. It does not matter if you are in Peking, Tientsin, Shanghai, England or the United States. Once you drop any object, it falls to the ground at once. Such, then, is what law is. Because it never changes, it is therefore called a law.

How does sin, generically speaking, become law? It is because there is a regular pathway or track to all our sinful acts. Every time people scold you, you feel unhappy within you. It does not matter if you are scolded in the morning or in the evening, today or tomorrow or the day following. On all three hundred and sixty-five days of the year, you will feel unhappy when scolded. The same is true that you feel elated when people praise you, that you feel high when praised on any and all of the three hundred sixty-five days of the year. The same emotional reaction happens on every one of the days of the year. So, too, is our sin a law, for every sin works in us the same. Our sin is something special. In the world there are all kinds of doctors, but I have never met a doctor of sin. It is because a person can commit the same sin or sins, but not all the sins. How strange it is that there is no new discovery in sin. It is always one or two sins which bother you and subdue you. A harsh person is harsh in all things and will not let go easily. A proud man is forever proud. A bad-tempered person will always lose his temper. Sin is a law to us. It controls us and causes us to commit the same sin over and over again. It is rare for anyone to commit one kind of sin today and another kind of sin tomorrow, and still another kind the day after that.

There is one kind of sin which each of us always commits. If one of us is twenty years old, that particular sin will have followed him for those twenty years. If one of us is fifty, the same sin will have bothered him for all of his fifty years. Unless we all are delivered, the same particular sin will follow us throughout our lifetime. And that is what Paul called the inward sin. Such sin cannot be resolved simply by forgiveness because a person commits the same sin after forgiveness. We each of us may be saved, but even after being saved, sin continues to follow us.

Even Paul had a sin (that of coveting) which followed him (cf. Romans 7:7c). In spite of his determination to forsake it, he continued to commit this sin. He mightily resisted, but he could not be delivered. Later on, he cried out, "Wretched man that I am! who shall deliver me out of the body of this death?" (Romans 7:24) The Romans had an extraordinary kind of punishment. If a man had killed another person, the dead body (Paul's "body of death") would be bound to the murderer, face to face, hands to hands, torso to torso, and feet to feet. When he sat, the corpse also sat. When he walked, the corpse would, too. Wherever he went, the corpse would be there with him. There was no way of escape. Paul declared that his sin was like a corpse which accompanied him every which way, because it was attached to him.

Do we realize that there is a kind of sin that, like a corpse, follows us all the time and every which way and gives us no rest? Unless we become aware of this, there can be no deliverance. For sure, God will cause us to see the evil of the sin nature in us—that it is as miserable as that attached corpse, and we must be delivered from it. Some people know forgiveness of sins through the blood, but they do not know there is a sin nature in them which compels them to do what they have detested doing repeatedly.

The Cross Deals with the Sin within Man

The Bible reveals two different ways for dealing with sin. The sin before God is to be solved by the blood; but the sin in the flesh is to be dealt with through the cross. The effects of the blood and the cross are totally different according to the Scriptures. Blood is for God, and it is outward and objective in its effect; cross is for men, it being inward and subjective in effect. The Bible only tells of calling people to be crucified with Christ; it has not called us to shed blood with Him. Let us understand that the outward sin is settled by Christ alone while man does nothing, whereas in dealing with the inward sin it depends on the power of the cross to eliminate the old man (Romans 6:6a).

Romans 6:6 mentions these three things: first, the old man; second, the body of sin; and third, bondage to sin. So, there are sin, old man, and body brought into view. How can we cease our being in bondage to sin? Sin is like a master who is highly influential. The word sin here is cast in singular number in both Greek and English. It therefore has reference to the sin within, an active force within to motivate and push a person to commit sins. Some have served sin for several decades without being freed. Even though it has sometimes been resisted, it always ends up in defeat. Sin is powerful, yet we cannot blame it for our sins. Who is to be blamed but our old man? This old man is that which is passed down to us from fallen Adam.

Do we recall how we sin? When we sin, we sense we should not sin, yet there is a force within us pushing us to do so. For instance, suppose someone says something unpleasant to you; something in you impels you to quarrel with him. Such is illustrative of how the sin within works in us: here you are, a Christian; for you to quarrel is not commendable, but you cannot help but quarrel for you feel suffocated within; and you feel released after you quarrel: so, within you there is a master who gives an order (your old man), the steward (your self or soul) agrees, and passes on the order to the body to carry it out.

Sin is but a force which impels you from within, but it is your old man who wills to sin. Once a brother told me that if he continued to be patient, his stomach would burst. This exemplifies how severe is the temptation within. One has an opinion, the other agrees. One feels compelled, and the other does it. Hence, the body is the organ to carry out the opinion or order; for without the body, no act of sin can be carried out. The body is therefore like a figurehead who does whatever is commanded of it. The Bible appropriately calls it the body of sin since all unrighteous acts come out of the body. It is the eyes of the body that focus upon unrighteous scenes; the brain which thinks up improper thoughts; the hands that perform evil acts; and the feet which walk to sinful places. Each and every sinful action is carried out by the body. Hence, the Bible tells us that it is the sin nature that proposes, the old man that agrees, and the body that executes. With the cooperation of these three, man commits sin.

THE WAY OF DELIVERANCE: CRUCIFY THE OLD MAN

How can we be delivered? The Holiness Christians among God's people claim that God has eradicated the root of sin, and hence the Christian will never sin again. The Chinese declare that since all bad acts are done by the body, then a person should ill-treat his body and control it till whatever is evil sees not, hears not, speaks not, and moves not; and thus the body is tightly bound. Unfortunately, this method does not work, for one may put one's body under the tightest control, but he cannot control his heart from thinking and proposing evil.

At one time there were two Christians living together. One was an aunt and the other was her niece. One day someone unjustly scolded the aunt. The aunt simply smiled, not having been stirred up outwardly at all. When the niece heard and observed all this, she greatly admired her aunt. After the scolder left, she said to her aunt, "Though he scolded you and not me, nevertheless, his scolding of you set my head on fire." "Do you really think," responded the aunt, "that I was not burning? The fire burnt fiercely within me also." Many assume that if they do not sin outwardly they are victorious. That is just not so.

God does not deal with the body of sin, nor does He crucify the root of sin. His work is not done outside the body; rather, He does His work inside the body by dealing with the old man. This old man likes to be a slave to sin, so God crucifies the old man. For sin tempts and compels, and the old man also loves to be slave to sin; and thus these two elements cause the body to sin. Paul said, "Knowing this, that our old man was crucified with him [Christ]" (Romans 6:6a). What is crucified is the old man. The verbal phrase "was crucified" is cast in the past tense, and hence, it is an event forever done. Our old man is not *going* to be crucified with the Lord, nor will it *be* crucified in the future; to the contrary, it is *already* crucified. When Christ was crucified on Calvary, our old man was included in His crucifixion. When Christ died, the old man died simultaneously with Him.

The Death and Resurrection of Christ (2)

Suppose a sinner wants to be saved tonight, so he prays to God, saying: "O God, have mercy on me! Please cause the Lord Jesus to shed His blood for me to redeem me of my sins." Were you to hear it, you would undoubtedly tell him that such prayer is wrong, for how can anyone ask God to cause the Lord to shed His blood? His blood has already been shed for the sinner. All the latter need do is ask God to give him faith to believe, for by faith the sinner will be saved. Instead of asking the Lord to shed His blood for him tonight in order to redeem him of his sins before God, the sinner must believe that His blood has already been shed. He need only believe and he will be justified. Likewise, faith must be exercised by the Christian towards this matter regarding the old man. Let us not ask God to crucify our old man, for the Lord has declared that the old man has already been crucified. Just as redemption and forgiveness are past events, so also is the old man crucified a past event.

If we believe in the forgiveness of our sin because the Lord himself has already made that possible, then the crucifixion of our old man is also already realized for us through believing that the Lord has already crucified our old man with Him. By looking at either the Greek or English translation of Romans 6:6a we know and are assured that the crucifixion of the old man is a past event—that our old man has already been crucified. Yet knowing this accomplished fact alone is not sufficient, it has to be believed as well. If we believe that our old man has been crucified, then we should praise God, declaring: "Praise Him, I am dead."

OLD MAN CRUCIFIED AND THE BODY UNEMPLOYED

Now as the old man was crucified, "the body of sin" was "done away" (Romans 6:6b). In the original Greek, the word translated in English as "done away" actually means "unemployed." Originally, the business of the body of sin is to sin. The mouth, for example, is for scolding people and the brain is for thinking up unclean thoughts. But if the old man has *died*, the mouth can no longer scold, nor the brain conjure up unclean thoughts. And thus both the mouth and the brain become unemployed. Although the sin within still impels you to sin, there is no longer the old man to respond, for the Lord's new life within you cannot sin because it has no love for sin. Hence the body is unemployed.

In Tientsin there was a man who loved to play cards. His two hands were naturally used to play cards. But after he believed in the Lord, his two hands were now unemployed. This is an illustration of what Paul has here declared: that once the old man within was crucified, the body without became unemployed. And thus a person is kept from sinning and is no longer a slave to sin. Although the sin within may tempt and temptation is still present, a dead person will not sense it and hence there is no reaction. Such, then, according to the Scriptures, is

The Death and Resurrection of Christ (2)

the effective work of the cross which can be every Christian's experience.

The efficacious work of the cross is totally different from that of the blood. The blood was shed by our Lord for the remission of sins before God. We absolutely have no part in it. For us to be crucified with Christ is not for sins, it is for getting rid of our old man. The Bible says that "the blood of Jesus his Son cleanseth us from all sin" (1 John 1:7b). This passage tells us that the blood of Christ is for cleansing us of our sins, but it does not say that the blood is for cleansing the old man, or for cleansing us, or for cleansing the flesh. That is because all these are dealt with by the cross (Galatians 2:20, 5:24). None of these is cleansed by the blood; rather, they are all crucified: "they that are of Christ Jesus have crucified the flesh with the passions and the lusts thereof" (Galatians 5:24). Here we can readily see that the flesh is not washed by the blood. Yes, our outward uncleanness can be washed with blood, but our inward flesh and old man cannot be so washed. Instead, the flesh and the old man must be crucified.

Every time the Bible speaks of the cross, it refers to self (or the flesh) and the old man. The cross in Scripture never points to sin. Sin needs to be washed with the blood, but the old man must be dealt with by the cross. Do we now see the Lord's full salvation here?

We all know that China today forbids the smoking of opium, and its supply in the possession of her citizens, if discovered by the governmental authorities, will be confiscated and disposed of. Opium comes from one or more secret opium factories and is those factories' sole product. Our old man can be likened to the opium factory. The latter can produce opium every day; so that even if the authorities are able to confiscate the factory's daily production of opium on any given day, the opium factory can still continue to produce more and more of its illegal product. In like manner, though our outside sin may be washed by the blood, soon afterwards our old man will nonetheless continue to commit sin. Hence, whereas the blood "confiscates," as it were, the sin committed outwardly, it is the cross which gets rid of the old man that commits the sin. The work of the cross cannot be likened to the authorities who dispose of the opium factory's daily supply of its product but likened to those who successfully bomb the factory to extinction. Once the factory has been destroyed, opium will not be produced anymore. Once the cross has eliminated the old man, sin can no longer be committed.

What is meant by the cross? We will recall that when the Jews rejected the Lord, they cried out: "Crucify him!" (John 19:6) This was followed by another cry: "Away with him" (John 19:15). The cross is a total putting away. They got rid of the Lord by using the cross. Similarly, today the Lord gets rid of our old man with the cross. Blood is for the remission of sins; cross is to rid us of our old man. Once our old man is gotten rid of, there is full salvation. Christ's blood is objective in its effect for the remission of our sins; cross is subjective in its effect for the elimination of the old man so that we can be emancipated from sin.

All issues of salvation are resolved on the basis of "faith." All the necessary works of salvation have been accomplished by God. His word tells us that we have been crucified with Christ (Galatians 2:20). Perhaps you do not have faith and hence doubt that there is such provision. You are still you; you do not feel any differently. But do please recall the event of your initial salvation: you as a sinner believed in the Lord's blood that washed away your sins, and you were instantaneously saved. So, also, as you now believe in the cross, you can immediately praise God, saying: "Thank God, my old man is dead!"*

---

*Note: Message given on 5 August 1937.

4: "Reckon"

"Even so reckon ye also yourselves to be dead unto sin, but alive unto God in Christ Jesus" (Romans 6:11).

RECKON OURSELVES AS DEAD IN CHRIST JESUS

Yesterday we came to understand the fact that God has already crucified our old man. What must we do, now that our old man has been crucified? The Bible tells us that we should reckon ourselves as being dead in Christ Jesus and our also being alive in Christ Jesus. Towards sin we reckon ourselves as being dead but towards God as being alive in Christ Jesus.

What does reckoning mean? We know that in the world our speech is often inaccurate and even our writings may be incorrect. We dare not say that what is recorded in history and in historical narratives are one hundred percent factual or even almost factual. What, then, is the one undertaking in the world which is most accurate? Is it not that of accounting? For example, two plus two is four. This accounting or reckoning is certain, for no one can declare that two plus two is three and be believed. No, the mathematical equation, two plus two equals four, can never be said to be less or more. For those in kindergarten the reckoning of two plus two being four is true just as it is for the college students in the world. Not because a person has a doctor's degree can that one credibly say that two plus two is five. Hence, accounting or reckoning is one of the most exact activities in the world.

Here God has accounted us as having died, for we were already dead. Just as you cannot say four is the answer to two plus two unless the answer is truly four, so you cannot reckon yourselves as dead unless you are truly dead. Suppose you are an accountant in a store. What can you do if the account shows a loss of twenty thousand dollars? You can only report such an amount as a loss. You cannot enter such an amount into the account book as being an *earning* of twenty thousand dollars. Whatever is recorded in the account ledger must be exactly whatever has been the loss or gain. Hence, when God reckons us to be dead, it means precisely that—that we have really died. Only real death can be reckoned as being dead. You cannot reckon yourselves as being dead if you have not yet died.

The call in the Bible for us to reckon is a call for us to experience faith. How do we reckon? We reckon by faith. We now know that when the Lord was crucified, He had brought our old man with Him to be crucified as well. This hopeless, sinful and defiled you was crucified with Him too. If you still consider yourselves as alive and not dead, let me tell you, this is because you have no faith.

"Reckon"

BELIEVE GOD'S WORD, NOT ONE'S FEELING

I often sense that what believers lack most is faith. We know the truth, but we lack experience. This is due to our lack of faith (Hebrews 4:2b). If there is living faith, all will be real. Without faith, truth remains truth and you remain you but there is no connection between the two. Yet with the exercise of faith, all the Biblical truths will become your experience. God has declared you are dead in Christ Jesus, you believe that declaration of fact, and so you are really truly dead.

Two years ago a foreign missionary came to see me. She was a sister in the Lord and had a few children. She said to me: "Mr. Nee, I am really at my wits' end. If one of my children cries I can bear it, but when another also cries, I lose my patience. My patience can only endure one, not two of them, crying. I lose my temper, Mr. Nee, so what can I do? I continue to see myself as really still alive, I not having died. This is the reason for my failures. Had I truly died, everything would be fine. Is that not so?" I answered her with a smile, saying: "Where in Scripture does God tell you that you died in yourself? God has never said that. What He *has* said is that you died *in Christ*. If your eyes only see yourself, you shall see that you are indeed very much alive. But if you see Christ, you will see that you truly did die."

Many Christians know the truth of co-death, but they still look at themselves and therefore feel themselves to be alive. God has never said that upon your hearing the truth of co-death and looking at yourself that you will therefore see yourself as dead. Such would be according to feeling, not according to faith. Faith is looking to Christ and not at oneself. Faith is seeing oneself in Christ, not seeing oneself in himself. Believers should never look at themselves; they should always view themselves as being in Christ.

Satan will continually tempt you by telling you that you are alive. How do you know you are alive? You know it in yourself. Satan therefore tempts you to look at yourself. He deceives you by saying to you that God has indeed said you died, but where, adds Satan, did you die? For being thus tempted by the enemy, you look at yourself and, alas, you see you have *not* died. What do you really believe? Do you believe God's word or believe your feeling? God says that I died in Christ. But Satan says I have not died; and when I look at myself, I see myself as not dead. After all is said and done, do I believe God's word or believe my feeling?

Such points up the difference between living faith and dead faith. You know you have said that you died. Do you believe the word of God or believe your feeling? Which is true—God's word or your experience? You should believe God's word, for that is what faith is. If you have living faith, you may look at yourself as alive but you are able to declare that though you feel alive you do not believe you are.

I trust in God's word, not in my feeling. God has said I died, hence I am dead. What therefore is living faith? It is

"Reckon"

taking hold of the word of God. Only His word is true. My feeling and experience may change, but I believe what God's word has made clear—that all the works which God has done in Christ have been accomplished.

Today's problem lies precisely here: we only see our being alive and let the word of God slip away from us: we hold onto our feeling within and cast away God's word without. Whenever our feeling and God's word are opposed to each other, we should believe God's word instead of believing our feeling. Then we are delivered. Countless believers have heard the truth of our co-death and co-resurrection with Christ, but most only know the truth without exercising living faith; and thus all becomes vain for them.

In this particular regard, how useless is our brain. For when temptation comes, our brain will commence thinking what we should do in order to die. Let me tell you that such action shows the lack of faith. The issue here is whether we can believe that we have already died in Christ. It is not a matter of us *going* to die; rather, it is a matter of believing we have *already* died: not what we can do, but accepting and believing that all has already been done: not how we can resist temptation but how we can believe God's word.

As was said earlier, if the store has earned money, the ledger will naturally reckon it as an earning. How, then, should I reckon if God has said I died? I should obviously reckon myself to be dead. Many believers acknowledge that all would be fine if only they had truly died. Well, the fact is that they *have* died, for in Christ all problems have indeed been solved. God never says I am going to die; rather, He declares that I have already died.

Unless I am truly dead, how can God instruct me to reckon myself as dead? On the other hand, if I have in fact not died, how, again, can God instruct me to count myself dead? If the store has lost money, how can the owner instruct the accountant to put it down in the ledger as an earning? Because I have truly died, God can cause me to reckon myself dead. God will never instruct me to make a false account. Thank God, I have truly died in Christ. It does not matter whether I have experienced it or not, the fact is that my old man has already died, for the work of Christ has been fully accomplished.

You must reckon yourself as dead, and with faith you shall experience it, but without faith you will not have any experience of it. If temptation comes and you are stirred to feel you are not dead, then at that moment you will either believe your inward feeling or believe the word of God. Whether you believe God or believe feeling will be demonstrated at that very moment. We must have faith in God, not look for proof. If only we believe in what God has said, there will be no need of proof.

A trustworthy person need not provide any proof. Suppose I lend money to the country's president; do I need any guarantee? But if I lend to a rickshaw driver, I will for sure need a guarantee of some kind should he flee away later. Simply by His word God need not provide a guarantee. What He says is final; but why?

"Reckon"

Because He is the most honorable Person in the universe. What He says as having been done is done indeed (cf. Hebrews 6:18a). My feeling tells me that I have not died and am still sinning. At that moment, what do you believe? Do you believe you died in Christ or believe you are alive on the basis of your feeling? All who believe they are dead in Christ are blessed, for all their problems are eternally solved.

Living faith is believing God's word. It is not a believing some doctrine, for doctrine in mind has no power. Believe the word of God, resist all which belongs to self, and simply trust that God has already done all which is necessary. So that when temptation comes and your heart is stirred up for you to be proud or unclean, to worry or be jealous, what should you do? Let me tell you that a man of faith is able to praise God and declare that even though he may worry, he is dead; that though he may lose his temper, he still is dead. Even if your feeling should be contradictory to God's word, you will still praise God for all which He has done in Christ. If you believe yourself to be in Christ, if you believe that you are truly joined to Him, then you will certainly leap and shout, "Thank God I am dead!"

The problem today lies in your seeing the truth but not seeing God's finished work; in your seeing the truth but not seeing what is the content of the truth. It is like studying geography but you have never been to the places you have read about. You need God's revelation, you need His light to shine on you. Then you will see your position in Christ. Since you have not seen, there is no way to believe. On the other hand, let us say that I go into a room and hide there; you can easily believe that I am in the room because you saw me going in. Today you cannot see you are dead; on the contrary, you see yourself as alive and your old man is still alive. But thank God, though you cannot see, yet you believe, for you have seen that you are united with Christ in one. Therefore, when He died, you died also.

Suppose there is a cold drink in this bottle I have here in my hand. And suppose I bring this bottle to the pier and throw it into the sea. We cannot say on the one hand that the bottle is in the sea but that on the other hand the cold drink is still back in the Y.M.C.A. or in brother Wong's home. Not so, for where the bottle is, there is the cold drink. Even so, God has put us in Christ; and since Christ has died, we who are in Him have died as well.

For Us to Be in Christ Is God's Will and by His Work

"Of him [God] are ye in Christ Jesus" (I Corinthians 1:30a). In other words, for you to be in Christ is the will and work of God. I may be a weak person, for my hands cannot lift eighty pounds; but I can pour water into a bottle. God is omnipotent. For Him to put me in Christ is easier than for me to pour water into a bottle. You being in Christ Jesus is God's will and by God's work. Hence,

"Reckon"

God's word declares that when Christ died, at that very moment you also died.

Two years ago I was conducting meetings in Kaifeng. As I was speaking of the believer being in Christ, one of those in attendance asked me: "How can I be in Christ? How is it that when Christ died, I too died? that when Christ lives, I too live?" I replied as follows: "For me to be in Christ is God's work. It is God who puts us in Christ, so, the experience of Christ becomes our experience. All God's works are done in Christ, not in us. This is the difference between Christianity and other religions. In all other religions, all works are done in man. Only in Christianity are works not done in man. In the Christian faith all are in Christ alone; so that if you are related to Christ, all Christ's experiences become yours. Without such relationship with Christ you remain as you are and the work of Christ has no effect on you."

I went on to explain to this inquirer at the Kaifeng meeting the following. Do you know how the electric bulb gives light? It gives light through the electric wire which is connected with the power plant. The power of light-giving is not in the bulb; rather, it is back in the power plant. Because the bulb is in touch with the power plant, it lights up. Remove the bulb from its contact with the power plant and it itself has no light, because it is the power plant which produces electricity, not the bulb. Similarly is the work of God. God conducts no work in man: all His works are done in Christ: death is in Christ and resurrection is also in Christ: all are accomplished in

Him. So that by having living faith which is in touch with Christ all God's works will be effective in you. Without that contact with Christ by exercising faith which is living you will remain your usual self. Therefore, the issue lies in whether or not you have faith. By faith you are able to be related to Christ. So you must believe in what God has done in Christ.

I continued explaining to this same inquirer as follows. By carefully reading the Bible you will come to realize that you can never change yourself; God has not said that He will change you. You will remain the same forever. Imagine a light bulb one day saying to itself: "I have been here for a long time; I shine forth light every day. I am sure I have light within me." But, then, suppose the bulb disconnects itself to see if there is still light shining forth. Naturally, there will no longer be any light coming forth, because whenever the bulb is disconnected from its source of electricity, it cannot give light anymore. In like manner, unless you are in contact with Christ, you will remain the same as you always have been. If there is no contact with Christ, you shall be like someone studying a book of geography without that person ever having visited the places he had been reading about. You may know the truth of co-death, but to experience being really dead is another matter. Without the illumination of the Holy Spirit, doctrine is useless and has no effect.

Even though I had responded to my inquirer this way, he still could not be convinced. So I continued by asking

"Reckon"

him the following: "Who is the ancestor of the Chinese?" "We Chinese," he replied, "are the descendants of Yellow Emperor." So I next asked: "Do you remember that on one occasion Yellow Emperor went forth to fight against Tsuyu?" "Yes, I remember," answered the inquirer. "Suppose Tsuyu had killed Yellow Emperor at that battle," I further said, "could we still be said to exist?" He answered me by saying: "If Yellow Emperor had died at that moment, with us not yet having been born, there would be none of us today." So I said to him in conclusion: "Exactly! Thus by your answer I see that you realize that the descendants of Yellow Emperor were in Yellow Emperor and that when he did eventually die, all his descendants died with him. Similarly, God has put us in Christ, and thus we are united with Christ. So that when Christ died, we died with Him; and when He arose, we too were raised up. We cannot say that, Christ having died on the cross, we are still alive. That is impossible. We are in Christ, so His experience is our experience."

Mere mental understanding of the doctrine of co-death with Christ and co-resurrection with Him is futile. May God give us light and revelation so that we may see and experience the fact that we are united with Christ in His death and in His resurrection: it is not only understanding the death mentally, it is also experiencing the fact of it, we realizing how we are united with Christ in one. Have we all therefore seen our place in Christ?

Nowadays, God's children pay much attention to doctrine but do not see what the context of a given doctrine is. Let us therefore not be content in merely knowing the various Christian doctrines. Let us additionally acknowledge that we only have an initial understanding, that we must seek for the enlightenment of the Holy Spirit so that we may know inwardly the reality of these doctrines—especially that of our being united with Christ. He who believes possesses it, he who reckons experiences it. God has said it and we possess it. May He grant us light that we may see that we are truly in Christ.

Only Believe and Praise

Hudson Taylor was a most spiritual person in Christ. Once he wrote to his sister and said that he did not know why he was always defeated without any victory. To say that he did not know the truth would be incorrect, for he actually knew it. But the result was that truth remained truth and he remained himself. There was no connection between the two. So he sought God earnestly, hoping that he might be connected to the truth in experience. Later on, Hudson Taylor wrote again to his sister, reporting to her that the scales had finally fallen from his eyes for, formerly, he had sought unsuccessfully to be in Christ: that he had used every means to put himself in but that he had always come back out: that he had found no way to get himself into Christ, all his attempts having been in vain. Praise God, however, for he now understood, having finally seen that he was already in

"Reckon"

Christ. It was no longer a matter of how to enter but how not ever to get out—how never to come out again. Hudson Taylor had at last seen that the Lord had said that He is the True Vine and we His disciples are the branches (John 15:5a). Therefore, we are already in Him and that He is ours and we are His—that there is no need in trying hard to be a branch but instead realizing that the believer in Christ has been born again as a branch.

Let us suppose that here is a person named Mr. Tang. He kneels down and earnestly prays, "O God, have mercy on me. Make me a Tang." God will say, "What? Are you not already a Tang?" Or to use another illustration, here is a flower pot that is ridiculously asking to be a flower pot. Just so, since we are already branches, there is no need to ask to be branches. Whatever God has said, it is already done. We have no need to pray but to praise. What is faith in regard to the truth of the believer's co-death and co-resurrection with Christ? It is a believing that you and I are already united with Christ. Therefore, let us praise God, for He has put us in Christ.

Do consider this, that you very well know that you are saved. You very well have the assurance because you believe that the Lord Jesus has shed His blood to redeem you of your sin. You had trusted, you had believed, and you accepted Christ and His salvation. Would you ever ask God to save you again? No, for you know that God has said in His word that whoever believes is saved. And you believed and know you are saved; and hence, you immediately praise God and declare that you are saved.

Likewise is it in this matter of our being united with Christ. We do not need to ask God to cause us to *be* united with Him, for all who belong to Christ are already united with Him. We simply need to believe in our having already been united, there being no need for prayer. If we believe that we have already been united with Christ, we naturally also believe that our old man died in Christ: there is no further need of our dying. The only need is for us to praise God. If you see that you are dead in Christ, then you shall see that sin has no power over you. When God says you are dead, it is true. Never ask for death anymore; for all has been done.

May God open our eyes, causing us to see that His work has already been accomplished. The blood has been shed. The cross has put old man Adam to death. All the negative work of redeeming us of Adam's fall has been achieved. For us, let us only believe. May God grant us light to see that all has been accomplished in Christ.[*]

---

[*] Note: Message given on 6 August 1937.

5: Living Faith

"Therefore I say unto you, All things whatsoever ye pray and ask for, believe that ye receive* them, and ye shall have them" (Mark 11:24).

Faith and Obedience

In these past few evenings we have been considering how the death and resurrection of Christ on the cross has four facets to His work. We have come to see the blood, the cross, the flesh, and the bearing of the cross. We have already considered at some length the first two facets: how Christ has redeemed us from sins and has also crucified our old man. These two facets, which are concerned with the blood and the old man, are both done *in Christ*. The other two, those of the flesh and cross-bearing, are to be done by Christ *within us*. So, the work of Christ can be divided between what is done in Him and what is done in us. John 15 says: "Abide in me, and I in you" (v. 4a). We can say that the first two facets of Christ's work are concerned with His word to "abide in Him" and the last two facets are related to His word, "I in you." Blood and crucifixion are those facets of His work which we know we have received in Christ, while what is

---

* Please note that the ASV has a marginal footnote that indicates: Greek: *received.—Translator*

later to be spoken about regarding the flesh and bearing the cross are those facets of Christ's work which He will do in us. For us to be in Christ needs our faith, and for Christ to do His work in us requires our obedience. Faith and obedience are the two most important spiritual exercises for Christians to engage in.

Faith is believing I am already in Christ, that I am already one with Him, that whatever is His is mine, that all His experiences I too have experienced. Thus, living faith is believing that whatever is Christ's is also mine. What Christ will do in us, however, requires not only faith but also obedience: we need to obey His leading. When the Lord works in us, sometimes it is an urging, at other times it is a forbidding. Sometimes we do not move when we should, so He will cause us to know what to do. At other times we are doing things in the flesh, and He will therefore check us within and cause us to sense that such things should not be done again. So the Lord frequently impels us or prevents us. To believe and obey is to listen to His moving and forbiddance. Oftentimes we sense within us a kind of soundless voice, a sort of senseless sense. We can neither see nor hear nor touch, but we seem to see, to know and to sense. Such inward motion causes us to know what should or should not be done. Hence, to be obedient is to obey that inner leading. Obedience is more than obeying the Bible; it is also obeying the inner leading. In order to have a victorious Christian life we must know what is obedience as well as what is faith. On the other hand, if there is neither living faith nor obedience, doctrinal truth will only be in the brain and not also in spiritual experience.

Christians must exercise faith to receive all that is in Christ, and they likewise need to exercise obedience to accept all that Christ will do in them. The way of victory is therefore twofold: one is faith and the other is obedience. The efficacy of the blood needs faith, not obedience, because blood is the work of Christ. All that is accomplished in Christ must be received by faith, not by obedience. The fact of the old man having been crucified is not to be obeyed but to be believed. Exercise faith to believe that you have already died in Christ.

Believe you have already received all things prayed and asked for, and you shall have them. This evening we shall see what living faith is. How can we possess all the riches in Christ? Everybody is familiar with this word "faith," yet much so-called faith is not genuine faith. Such faith produces nothing. For instance, the Bible tells us that our old man has already died and many Christians declare that they believe this; nevertheless, their faith has no effect upon their Christian walk. Let us therefore search the Scriptures and learn what faith really is. Let us first acknowledge that what many people's faith is, is but a consent of the mind; it is not a believing in the heart. Their brains may approve of a teaching or preaching as being reasonable and good. However, let us never consider this to be faith. The mind's acceptance of someone's teaching or preaching as being good or reasonable is not necessarily believing the truth.

What is faith? Let us listen to what the Lord has said: "All things whatsoever ye pray and ask for, believe that ye received them [past tense], and ye shall have them." This is the only place in the whole Bible that tells us what faith is. Indeed, this is the one place in the entire Bible which tells us how to believe. The Romanized Amoy Bible is even more accurate in translating the Greek verb for the English word "received" as "already received." Believe you have already received and you shall have.

So what is faith? Faith is believing I have already received. It is not believing I shall, I will, or I must receive but is believing I have received already. Just in case you have not grasped how great is the difference here, let me explain further that if a person only believes he shall or will receive, such faith is faulty. Only one kind of faith is true; namely, that when you believe, you believe you have already received. This kind of faith shall receive God's promise. What enables God to give us all the riches of Christ arises from the exercise of such faith. Today's problem lies in the fact that many of God's children claim they have faith, they believing they *shall* receive. Yet those who have believed in this fashion for millions of times have failed to receive. For God does not deem this kind of faith to be true faith. He will not hear it. One kind of faith alone is acceptable to Him. The words "have already received" are most important. Believe that we have already received, and we shall have. Otherwise, merely *expecting* to receive is not faith at all.

The Faith That Saves

Let me illustrate this matter factually in order to help us to see that by believing that we have received we shall have. Let us suppose that here is a sinner, and that you share the gospel with him, showing him that he is a sinner and how Jesus Christ has accomplished the work of redemption for him. After talking to him at length, you want to know whether he has believed. So you ask him, and he replies that he wants to believe and to receive the Lord's forgiveness of his sins in order henceforth to be able to approach God through having trusted in the Lord Jesus. When you hear this, you are initially overjoyed, for you apparently have a gospel fruit.

You then ask him to pray asking for God's forgiveness of his sins. So he prays: "O God, please forgive my sins for I am a sinner who should be condemned. Thank You for causing the Lord Jesus to die for me and to shed His blood for me. I pray, for Christ's sake, that You forgive my sins and cause me to be a saved person." What would you think of such a prayer? Nothing could be better. If a person should pray such a prayer, he would most surely have passed the "gospel test," for such is considered to be a good standard prayer.

However, the fact of the matter turns out not to be so, because as you kneel by his side and ask him if his sins are now forgiven, his answer is as follows: "I believe God will save me; God will forgive my sins." Alas, you shiver at the two times of his saying "God will"—for he has said he believes that God will forgive him of his sins and save him. Can it be said that this man has been saved? All of us should realize that his sins have not been forgiven, that he is not yet saved. For his faith only extends to the point of "will." He thinks he fully believes, but actually he has not believed.

Then what is the true expression of faith here? It is expressed when, having been asked of him after his prayer if his sins have been forgiven, this sinner answers by saying, perhaps even with tears: "Thank God, my sins have been forgiven because of Christ. Thank God, I am saved." That is true faith being expressed. Faith is not a believing that one's sins "may" or "shall" be forgiven but a believing that one's sins *have* been forgiven. True faith is not a believing that you shall or will be saved, but a believing you *have* been saved. Such is the only kind of faith which the Bible gives us.

What, then, is faith? Faith is not believing what *shall* nor *will* be done; true faith is believing what *has* been done. How strange that many know what faith is when they are saved: they having believed that they had in fact been saved rather than that they will or shall be saved. But when it comes to this second truth of truths, they relinquish their former faith. At the time of salvation they knew they were saved through faith. But in the second stage of truth, they only believe they *shall be* delivered. Too many Christians, having learned the lesson of faith once, have lost their faith when it comes to the other work of Christ.

DELIVERANCE THROUGH FAITH

Let us see how we are to be delivered from sin. Six years ago someone came to meet with us. He was head of the trustees of a native Christian gathering. He was quite sick at heart. Nine-tenths of the salary of this group's pastor came from him. He was not only one who gave much, he was also very zealous for the Lord. He often came to our Bible study.

One Sunday morning he came to my home. I asked him if there was anything I could do for him. As I asked, his tears fell down. I asked him to tell me why. He said the following: "Mr. Nee, you do not really know me. You think I am zealous and love the Lord. Yet you do not truly know what kind of person I am. Although I am indeed zealous and love the Lord, I have a problem—my temper: simply over a little matter I will instantly leap up and angrily throw things around. I really feel bad afterwards. How can a Christian behave in such a way? I ask for the Lord's forgiveness. But when, soon after I pray, I see my staff do something wrong, I repeat doing the same thing. Even with my family, I treat them similarly. I am a Christian, but I act in such horrible manner. Although I know my sin, and even after I confess, my temper flares up again anyway."

He continued by saying: "I have a number of employees in my store; I tell them to work on Sunday and their Sunday work is to attend the Sunday church service. Yet because of my bad temper which I lose once or twice every day, they refuse to believe in the Lord. I preach the gospel to them; secretly, however, they say among themselves: 'He believes the Lord and is a Christian, but he is not any better than others; so why should we believe?' When I hear this, I am deeply troubled, for I shall be the cause of their eternal death. I ask God for forgiveness and determine not to lose my temper again. Alas, however, there is no improvement. My temper again goes out of control. For example, last night I quarreled so loudly that all my neighbors heard me. Over a tiny matter I threw things around in the store, even breaking the glass window. For me, to lose money is a small thing; what troubles me most is the word of my employees, who say: 'How can a Christian be so bad?'"

He still went on, saying: "I knew my sin and I could not sleep last night. I do not like losing my temper, but I do it again and again. Today is the Lord's day. It happens that this morning is my turn to speak. I tell myself today that I must not lose my temper, for if I do, I will not be able to speak. A little while later, my wife brought me a hot soup. She herself could tolerate the heat, but I could not. So I got angry and threw the bowl at her. I have quarreled and consequently today's sermon is gone."

"I am a Christian," he continued, "but my temper is devilish. What can I do? I come to you today for this reason—please, Mr. Nee, think of some way to help me. Whatever way, help me to get rid of my temper."

As he spoke, I could tell he was truly grieved. But as I listened I began to laugh. He said, "Mr. Nee, you must help me, anyway." He was now crying. Yet the more he cried, the more I laughed. So he said, "Mr. Nee, I am so miserable." In reply I said: "Yes, you are miserable, but I am glad." "I am helpless," he cried. "There can be nothing better," I responded. "Mr. Nee, please do not joke with me."

I countered with the following words of explanation: "I said to you that I am glad over this development because the Lord is able to heal this kind of disease. Concerning other diseases some are able to cure themselves and others get well through doctors, but such a disease as yours only the Lord can cure. You shall know that the Lord will heal you. Yes, you sense your bad temper, but I see that the Lord is greater than your temper. He can heal you instantaneously." "How can it be so easy?" he asked; "you have not seen my temper. Had you seen it, you would realize that it is not so easy to heal." But I repeated to him: "Even if your temper were ten times worse, the Lord is able to heal you at once." I assured him of this again.

I now asked him to read Romans 8:2. Then I asked him what this word of God says there. He replied that God has said that the law of the Spirit of life in Christ Jesus made us free from the law of sin and death. So I asked him where the Holy Spirit made him free from the law of sin and death. He answered, "In Christ." I therefore said to him: "If you yourself are truly in Christ, what does the Bible say here? It says that the Holy Spirit in Christ sets you free from sin. In your case, what is the sin? It is your temper. The Holy Spirit in Christ has set you free so that you are delivered. Why is it, then, that you are still undelivered?" He answered, "Oh, today, I hope God will set me free." I continued by asking him: "Does the Bible tell you that the Holy Spirit *shall* set you free? No, what God says here is that the Holy Spirit in Christ Jesus *made* you free. What does the word 'made' mean? This verb 'made' is cast in the past tense. It thus means that the deed being described has been accomplished already in the past. Which is reliable, God's word or your word? Do you think God would lie?"

In response he said that he would never take God's word as being a lie. He believed in the word of the Bible. Yet he had not been delivered. So I pointed my finger at him and told him that God would never be afraid of his temper, even if it were ten times worse. I went on to say that the sin he had committed this morning surpassed all the sins he had ever committed through the years. "This morning," I said to him, "you committed the greatest sin—the sin of unbelief. There is no sin greater than that. You have the wicked sin of unbelief in you. Ask God to remove this wicked sin of unbelief from you which will enable you to believe."

I then told him that I myself had to speak today. "I must be quiet for awhile. So I must now go upstairs and I shall leave the sitting room to you for you to remain here and ask God for forgiveness and ask Him to remove this wicked heart of unbelief from you so that you can be delivered. Then ask God to deliver you that you might believe Romans 8:2." Accordingly, I went upstairs and after half an hour I came down and inquired how he was. He replied, "Mr. Nee, everything is now fine. I am completely delivered. I am truly set free." Praise God, he went back home rejoicing.

This man's faith which he had exercised that morning is an example of living faith. This man himself could not rid himself of his bad temper. That morning he truly believed and he was delivered. I was not to see him again thereafter for almost two months. One day, however, I met him on a trolley car and asked him how the matter was. He said, "Praise God, I am still free!" Another six months passed. I then saw him again, and again I asked how he was. He once more said, "Thank God, I am still delivered." Two years later, I met him in Hong Kong. I was able to remember him and inquired again how he was. Once more he replied, "Thank God, I am delivered."

What, then, is true faith? It is not believing that God *will* do, but in believing God has already done. The "made" in this Bible passage speaks of a past accomplished fact. Let us never change the "made" to "will be" or "shall be." Let us instead thank God that in Christ He has already set us free.

Healed through Faith

In 1929 I was in Foochow. Where I lived was about a two-hours' boat ride from the city. At that time we had among us a sister in the Lord who had a serious eye disease. So she had gone to Foochow for treatment. The doctor there told her that her eye was in such serious condition that even after her recovery she would need to wear glasses. The doctor agreed to treat her eye on a daily basis and would soon provide a pair of glasses for her.

Soon after this she heard me speak on faith. She believed, and she also prayed before God, saying: "My eye problem is very serious. I will need to go to Foochow every day hereafter for treatment. And even after I am recovered, I will have to wear glasses for life. Not only will this cost money, it will also be time-consuming." So she asked God for His healing. After she prayed she believed that God had healed her eye. So her heart was at peace and joyful.

However, she had already set up the next appointment with the doctor. What should she do now? A Christian should not violate an appointment and a person was obviously not going to be able to sell one's prescription glasses to others. So she went anyway. The doctor applied medicine to her eye and supplied the glasses to her. As she was returning on the steamer she thought in her heart that since she had believed in God's promise and God had already healed her eyes, what— she asked herself— should she do with the glasses and the medicine? In her mind came the thought that she would take the glasses and the medicine home and observe the situation regarding her eyes for a few days. In case she was not healed she could yet use them. But there came a counter voice within her, saying: "Have you believed that God has already healed you?" "I do indeed believe. What, then, can these things do for me?" But Satan said to her: "You should not take action too quickly. You have already spent quite a lot of money." Now she knew it was Satan's voice. So she began to praise God and threw the medicine and the glasses into the river. She was full of joy. She would later testify that she had never been so happy as she was at that moment. A week later her eyes were as well as anybody else's. One day, during the church assembly, she stood up and testified regarding her experience.

A few days afterwards I heard another story. A Christian brother's eyes had a problem. He went to the same doctor whom the sister had consulted. The doctor gave him medicine as well as spectacles. On that very day he had listened to the testimony of that sister. So, on his way back on the steamer, he told himself that since God had healed her, He could and would heal him too. "She had believed God, I have also believed God, who is not partial. He certainly can heal me." So with this kind of faith, he cast the medicine and the spectacles into the river. Upon his return he told his story to our brother Faithful Luke, stating that God would heal him.

One day shortly after this, brother Luke came to me and told me how the faith of such and such a brother had greatly improved. When I heard it, I said: "That sister's eye disease has really been healed, but I dare not guarantee this brother's healing." Brother Luke asked why. I replied that he had better take that brother to the doctor. Brother Luke thought that I was being too hard on him. But I said to him that it was because that brother did not have faith. Brother Luke said to me: "But he threw away those things that were worth more than twenty dollars, and he also stopped visiting the doctor. Are not these indications of faith?"

It so happened, however, that four weeks later the eyes of that brother had gotten worse. So he came to see me and asked me why God had healed that sister but not him. I told him that he had thrown away those things for his eyes too quickly, for he had not had faith. But he replied, "I do believe that God is able to heal me. Also God wants me to go to Kodiem to preach the gospel, and at my return He without doubt will heal me." So I told him to come see me after his return. Yet when he came back from Kodiem he was still not healed. I need to report that from 1929 up till today 1937 he has needed to wear a high-degree pair of spectacles and is still visiting the doctor. Why is this so? It is due to his lack of true faith.

Living Faith

Have Living Faith towards God's Word

Living faith is not believing that God *will* heal me; rather, it is believing that God has already heard my prayer. Whenever you believe that God has already heard you, your prayer has already been answered. That brother with the eye problem had believed from the first day that God *would* heal him, but that was of no effect. The Bible tells us of only one kind of faith: believe that you have received whatever things you have prayed and asked for and you shall have them. To believe that things asked for of God will or shall or can, comes from ourselves. Let us realize that, in this particular context, such words as "shall," "will," "able" and "can" are inappropriate, even negative, words. Living faith has nothing to do with such words. The words conveying living faith are "has been," "is" and "already." Hence, whatever is related to Christ, let us see that just as you believed and were saved, so now you believe and you are victorious; for all the riches of Christ—whether the baptism in the Holy Spirit, the power of the Holy Spirit, the healing of sickness, and all other blessings from above—are all yours.

Whenever you have God's word and you lay hold of it, believing that this word is yours, then that word belongs to you. Faith without God's word is false faith: it is useless and has no effect. Faith must have the word of God. Romans 8:2 and 6:6a are two of God's words. If we lay hold of God's words and believe them we shall already have the benefit of them.

The Lord Jesus said, "All things whatsoever you pray and ask for." How inclusive is this word? It includes everything: all the promises of God, all His abundant blessings, and all His accomplished facts. So simply believe that you have received them and you shall have them. May God give us light and cause us to know what living faith is. With such faith, all our difficult problems are solved. This, then, is the first lesson we must learn, and such shall be useful throughout our entire Christian life. May God bless us.*

---

* Note: Message given on 7 August 1937.

6: The Revelation on the Mountain

"And he said to them, Verily I say unto you, There are some here of them that stand by, who shall in no wise taste of death, till they see the kingdom of God come with power. And after six days Jesus taketh with Him Peter, and James, and John, and bringeth them up into a high mountain apart by themselves: and he was transfigured before them; and his garments became glistering, exceeding white, so as no fuller on earth can whiten them. And there appeared unto them Elijah with Moses: and they were talking with Jesus. And Peter answereth and saith to Jesus, Rabbi, it is good for us to be here: and let us make three tabernacles; one for thee, and one for Moses, and one for Elijah. For he knew not what to answer; for they became sore afraid. And there came a cloud overshadowing them: and there came a voice out of the cloud, This is my beloved Son: hear ye him. And suddenly looking round about, they saw no one anymore, save Jesus only with themselves" (Mark 9:1-8).

Revelation on the Mountain Causes Us to Know the True Image of the Lord

We are all quite familiar with this passage of Scripture. In the days of His sojourning on earth the Lord Jesus was clothed with flesh. He is the Son of God, and He now becomes the Christ of God—that is, the Anointed of God sent to earth on a mission. How can we explain this? As to His person He is the only begotten Son of God; and according to His work He is also the Christ of God. Matthew 16 tells us that He is both the Son of God as well as the Christ of God (v. 16), for the Son of God alone can be the Christ of God. He originally is the Son of the living God, full of glory, position and authority. But when the Word became flesh (John 1:14a), He came to the world as it were in disguise; and in His flesh people could not see Him as the Son of God. They only saw Him as a sibling to his half-brothers in the flesh named Simon, Judas, Joses and James (Mark 6:3). Furthermore, John the Baptizer was His flesh-and-blood cousin. So people could only see Jesus in the flesh and thus they could never understand the other reality which lay behind His flesh. Men knew Him only as Jesus of Nazareth and even questioned whether anything good could come out of Nazareth (John 1:46a). Therefore, unless people receive revelation of the Holy Spirit, they cannot more fully see Jesus.

Who is Jesus? He is the Son of God in disguise. What, in this context, does disguise mean? It means taking upon oneself another fashion or appearance than what one originally is. The Word becoming flesh was a disguise of the Son God. By taking on flesh, God the Son disguised himself. Hence, people saw the disguising flesh and did not recognize Jesus as the Son of God. People could see Him, touch Him, hear Him, eat with Him, and even preach and cast out demons with Him; yet they could not recognize Him as the Christ. They even could call

The Revelation on the Mountain

Jesus, Rabbi, as in the case of the rich young ruler and the religious teacher Nicodemus (Matthew 19:16-22, John 3:1-12). They could witness His personal relationship with God, yet they could not discern who Jesus really is.

Moreover, when Jesus asked His disciples who did men say that He was, they answered that some said Elijah, others said Jeremiah (Matthew 16:14). Why did they not say He was Daniel or Zechariah? Most likely it was because among all the Old Testament prophets, there was no one stronger than Elijah: how he had condemned all who opposed God: how he had battled with the ungodly prophets of Baal and overcame them all (I Kings 18:16-40). How about Jeremiah? He was a most tender person whom people called the weeping prophet, for whenever he confronted situations beyond his power to cope he cried.

So on the one hand, people said that Jesus was Elijah, for He hated sins so strongly; but on the other hand, other people saw Him weep for sinners, the poor, and Jerusalem—and so they said Jesus was Jeremiah. Though they seemed to know Him as the One who was better than the rest, yet all they could recognize Him to be was a prophet like Elijah or Jeremiah. Men knew only the outward appearance, they having seen Jesus' relatives, His daily work, and something of His human character; nevertheless, they did not in the least recognize Jesus for who He truly is.

There came a day, however, that Jesus took Peter, James and John up a mountain and there He was transfigured before them: His garments became white and His countenance shone as the sun. What did this mountain-top experience signify for these disciples? It was Jesus revealing His original self to these men. He at this moment was divesting himself of that outward disguise which had prevented people from recognizing His true nature. Moreover, when Jesus was transfigured atop the mountain, He was not changed into what He was not but was changed into what He originally is. Thus people could recognize Him as He really is—the eternal Son of God.

The Church Is Built on the Knowledge of the Revelation of Christ

The Bible tells us that the church is built on what Jesus termed "this rock" (Matthew 16:18). The Roman Catholic Church considers Peter to be the rock of that phrase of the Lord's. Actually it is a misreading of Scripture, for in the relevant Bible passage the word "Peter" in the original Greek means "stone" or "a small stone." And thus Jesus had said to Peter, "You are a stone, and upon this rock I will build my church." Can we therefore see that the church is not built upon Peter but upon "this rock"?

Now what is the meaning of "this rock"? People, in recognizing Jesus as the Christ and as the Son of the

The Revelation on the Mountain

living God—thus signifying both the work and the person of Jesus, have rightly concluded that this very affirmation is the rock. Hence, "this rock" refers to the revealed Christ. Knowing Jesus as both Christ and Son of the living God is not that which has been revealed by men but is only revealed by the Father who is in heaven (v. 17b).

All who only hear the Lord from men and merely know something *about* Him are not Christians. Whoever is not built on the rock are not in the church. Today everybody may receive revelation. Knowing Jesus in His person and work does not come from what men say of Him but must arise from a personal and direct recognition of Him. Many who read the Bible or listen to sermons remain unchanged because such activities are men's work and not God's. The work of God is to reveal His Son. Each and every would-be Christian must himself receive revelation from God; then he will know who Jesus truly is and with living faith accept Him as Lord. In this way each person will have a relationship with God. To know God and to know Jesus as the Lord is what a Christian is.

A person must not solely take notice of Jesus' outward appearance and thus classify Him as merely one among the ranks of the prophets Elijah and Jeremiah. One needs to know Jesus in the depth of one's heart. And it is this which makes a person a Christian. All who have not ascended the mount of transfiguration do not actually know the Lord Jesus. The problem today is in people knowing only the outward appearance of Jesus but not the *inward* Man. People may have read or been exposed to questions and answers concerning Christian truth, but they are still ignorant of the Bible and of Jesus. Their knowledge of Him is merely outward and is for the most part useless. He is to be known inwardly, that is to say, He must live in a person. True Christians look through His outward appearance and see His inward nature and character. Others may only observe the appearance, but Jesus' followers know His inside and thus have direct relationship with Him. Here, then, lies the difference between Christians and the world: all Christians will have ascended the mount of transfiguration, otherwise they will simply be traditional Christians or Christians in name only. They do not know the inward Lord.

What is being a traditional Christian or a Christian only in name? Let me use an illustration. Suppose there is a pastor's son here who reads the Bible morning and evening, prays, and is well acquainted with Bible stories. Fifty-two weeks of every year he attends a church service. Moreover, he is well acquainted with the teaching of Christianity and knows all his pastor-father's sermons. Nevertheless, he is not saved; indeed, he does not know how to accept Jesus as his Savior and thus his way is that of a traditional Christian. Whatever he has learned or acquired regarding Jesus has come from men and not received directly from God.

But thank God, one day the illumination of the Holy Spirit comes to this pastor's son. He himself has now met the Lord Jesus and formed a direct relationship with Him. He now truly knows the Lord. Such is the difference between knowing Jesus inwardly or only outwardly. Sadly, many so-called Christians only see the disguised Jesus and not His real self. But once they receive revelation and perceive His true image, they will have come to truly know Him.

Let me inquire, How do you know Jesus? If you know Him in the very depth of your heart, you have died and risen together with Him, and His victory is yours. Jesus Christ in you is a reality, an actuality that is nothing vague or obscure. May I say frankly that whoever has not the revelation of seeing Jesus as the Christ the Son of God is not a true Christian. He has no relationship with "the rock" and is thus an outsider.

Jesus asked His disciples one day, "Who do men say that the Son of man is?" We need to know the revealed Christ, and to believe and receive Him with living faith. If so, that will show that the kingdom of God has come to us. Without being born again no one can enter the kingdom of God, but those who have received revelation on the mount have entered the kingdom. Those who do not have revelation of the mount have not been born again, and hence, they have no part in the kingdom.

Romains 14:17 tells us: "the kingdom of God is not eating and drinking, but righteousness and peace and joy in the Holy Spirit." All things spiritual are in the Spirit. A person who has not received revelation from the Holy Spirit with regard to knowing Jesus knows nothing of spiritual things. If you commence talking to him of spiritual things, he will begin to develop a headache, for all things shared with him mean nothing to him. He has not seen God, not known Christ, and would never understand the things pertaining to God's kingdom. He may consider himself well-informed, yet all he knows is merely outward. So for him the Lord Jesus is but a misunderstood personality. The problem today lies in the fact that what the Christ is whom many children of God know is not sufficient. Permit me to say that knowing the true Christ does not come from knowledge and words of a pastor or teacher; on the contrary, one must himself receive light and revelation directly from God. This is the primary requirement in a genuine Christianity.

Law and Prophets Have Passed Away

Jesus ascended to a higher place: the mountain summit. If we see Him as the Christ of God, this will be revelation. When Jesus was transfigured atop the mount, He revealed His true self. There the three disciples recognized His true inward identity. They also saw Moses and Elijah with Jesus. Peter was one who liked to speak. Let us acknowledge that there are many descendants of Peter today; indeed, in the church there are many who like to speak. In speaking as he did on this occasion, Peter did not know what he was saying. Yet he could not keep quiet under such great revelation. On the

The Revelation on the Mountain

one hand he saw the true image of Jesus as Christ the Son of God, and on the other hand he also saw the most important figures in Judaism; in such a situation as that, how *could* this disciple of Jesus remain quiet? So Peter suggested to his Master to allow him to build three tabernacles: one for Thee, of course, but also one for Moses and one for Elijah (Mark 9:5b). In Peter's mind Jesus was the greatest of the three, so naturally He should have the first place. After Him there were the second and third positions. So let them be given tabernacles as well. To all this the Gospel writer's comment was that Peter "knew not what to answer" (v. 6a).

We Christians know, of course, that Moses represents law; and Elijah, the prophets. According to Peter's mindset Jesus the Christ was the center, but both law and prophet also had their places. Yet God did not think so, for such understanding would destroy the faith of future believers in Christ. Consequently, God in heaven immediately expressed His thought, for He instantly overshadowed the three disciples with a cloud and also dismissed Moses and Elijah. So that when the disciples looked about, they saw only Jesus. At the same time they heard a voice from heaven, saying, "This is my beloved Son: hear ye him" (vv. 7-8). In so many words God was telling them that this was no time for them to speak but only to hear—not what they might wish to suggest but what His beloved Son would be moved to say; therefore, hear Him.

To be a Christian is by inwardly recognizing who Jesus Christ truly is; it is certainly not by knowing the law and the prophets. For, firstly, law calls for outward regulation: it is that which is written on stones: it tells people what to do and what not to do and establishes an outward standard of right and wrong. Many Christians sense the leading of the Holy Spirit but they have not learned how to obey His leading. Instead, they follow what men say is right or wrong. Perhaps these Christians do see what the Bible says as to what is right or wrong, but they do not have inward revelation and thus have not learned how to follow the guidance of the Holy Spirit.

Add the Holy Spirit's Leading to the Bible's Teaching

A brother once asked me: "If I am to do a certain thing, please tell me what the teaching of the Bible is." I answered him in the name of the Lord with these words: "If you do not know the Bible's teaching on a particular matter, do you not have other means by which to know God's will?" During the Old Testament period there were only written rules void of any leading of the Holy Spirit within them. In the present New Testament period, however, we have the Holy Spirit indwelling us to lead us into doing God's will. In comparing today's New Testament era with that of the Old Testament we can say that whereas the Holy Spirit is living, the law is dead.

The Revelation on the Mountain

It is highly harmful to one's spiritual life if a person sees only rules and lacks the inward guidance of the Holy Spirit. In Old Testament times God's people had only the Judaic Scriptures without possession of the Holy Spirit within; but in our current New Testament era we also have the indwelling Holy Spirit who tells us what is right and what is wrong.

Today if anyone should look solely to the teaching of the Bible without also experiencing the Holy Spirit's guidance in relation to its teaching, that person is still living under the Old Testament dispensation and not under that of the New Testament. I am not in any sense despising the Bible; rather, what I am trying to say here is that while the Bible is without doubt most precious, it cannot be superior to the work of the Holy Spirit within the believer. In fact, if the New Testament is superior to the Old Testament, which it is, then the Holy Spirit surpasses the Bible. Some Christians deem the not keeping of the Ten Commandments to be against the law. They do not realize that the law is only a principle, apart from which it does nothing further. Yes, it tells us yea and nay, but nothing more. I would here declare that the Bible is indeed a most precious book, but it cannot be a substitute for the Holy Spirit nor is it the only standard against which a given action is to be judged as being right or wrong. The Bible is essential, but Bible truth must be supported by the leading of the Holy Spirit in relation to that truth.

Once a brother who fellowshiped with us talked about baptism with another brother who happened to be in the denominations. I would have to say that this brother of ours acted as though he were a member of the Baptist Church, since he talked about nothing but water baptism. He was able to convince that other brother regarding baptism by immersion. So he brought that other brother to my dwelling place and asked me to baptize him. I therefore asked that other brother why he wanted to be baptized. He said it was because he now saw that the Bible teaches immersion, not sprinkling. I then asked if he had prayed about it or had been led by the Holy Spirit in coming to his decision. His answer was, "The Bible says immersion; hence, I want to be immersed." I said to him: "You must go home. I am not going to baptize you because you have not received any revelation on this matter." This, then, is an example of following law.

Brethren today must realize that we are here not only to help people obey the Bible but also obey Bible truth through the Holy Spirit. I am not in any way denigrating the Bible. I simply maintain that to the Bible must be added the work of the Holy Spirit in the believer. For the Bible void of the Holy Spirit is the law. What is needed today is not law but having the living Christ dwelling in us in order that we might have His leading by means of God's Spirit. The Bible is not just law, though many do consider it as simply law—as *the* standard for determining whatever is right or wrong. This is a matter

The Revelation on the Mountain

of life and death, and is the difference between Judaism and Christianity. If we be unclear of this difference, how can we expect a great revival, for example, in the Chinese south sea area such as Singapore, the Philippines, and so forth?

Serving in the house of a medical doctor in Chefoo there was a maid. Once she came to Shanghai and got saved. She noticed that sisters had head coverings. She asked why and was told that it was done in obedience to the teaching of the Bible. Upon hearing this she began wearing a head covering as other sisters were doing. When she returned home she did the same; so her Christian mistress asked her why. She really did not know why, so she simply answered that the Bible taught head covering, and because the other sisters had their heads covered, she also did the same. Other than that, she knew nothing more. One day I came to this new sister's Chefoo home, and her mistress told me the story of her maid's head covering. I requested to have her brought to me immediately. She came, and I told her the following: "I am a representative of the church in Shanghai, and I wish to tell you that you should not have your head covered for the reason you stated because we do not have any sister who observes head covering for the reason you have explained. For the basis of your practice of head covering is law."

Let us be clear on this, which is, that outside rules and regulations can turn the most spiritual text—the Bible—into a deadening book of law. One day God had said to

Peter, "Listen to My Son; never mind the law and the prophets." What God had told Peter He also tells the whole church. Thank God! Christ Jesus lives not only in heaven, He also lives today in you and me. We do not listen to law alone, we should also listen to the leading of the living Christ in relation to that law.

We must now address the matter of the Old Testament prophets as represented by Elijah, who had also appeared on the mount with Jesus. Law is dead rule whereas prophets are living persons. Law cannot be put forth as the standard for every human act, word, movement or expression of behavior. You cannot find in the law that which is to govern what I am going to eat this evening, whether that be rice or congee or something else. Nor can it define how the church here in Singapore should meet. You cannot find these matters being determined in the law, since its coverage is limited. What the law has regulated is good, yet it is comprised of no additional rules for governing many other matters. That is why during the Old Testament era, there was not only dead law but also living prophets. For concerning whatever matter or issue which could not be found in the law you asked the prophets to inquire of God about on your behalf. The prophets were remedial agents who could and did fill up what was lacking in the law. You could not ask God yourself but you could request the prophet to ask Him for you. And then the prophet would relate to you what God had said.

The Revelation on the Mountain

Permit me to say that simply to be relieved or released from the Ten Commandments does not constitute being liberated from the law, since all outward regulations fall within the scope of the law. On the other hand, whatever command comes forth from the mouth emanates from the prophet. Back then, you yourself did not inwardly know God's will, so you asked the prophet to inquire for you. Thank God, not only the representative of the law—Moses—must be dismissed, even the prophets—as represented by Elijah—had to be dismissed, too. On the Mount of Revelation, not just Moses had to depart but even Elijah also had to disappear from the scene. As we have seen, the work of a prophet back then had been, among other responsibilities, that of seeking God's will for others. But the era of both the law and the prophets has now passed away. Today, with the prophets having been dismissed, we Christians cannot depend upon others to seek God for ourselves.

During New Testament Time All Know God Directly

What is the New Covenant or Testament? "The earth shall be full of the knowledge of Jehovah" (Isaiah 11:9b). You yourself can approach God and ask of Him directly. There is no need for the believer to consult his neighbor or seek out the prophet, for each and every person can now know God's will directly (see Jeremiah 31:33-34,

Hebrews 8:10-11). I have received many letters in the past year asking me for guidance about many matters. It is as though these letter-writers are saying, We have Mr. Nee as our prophet, so we need not go and inquire of God directly; let Watchman Nee tell us God's thought and will after he has inquired of Him. Brethren need to recognize that such behavior is of the Old Covenant way of seeking out a prophet. It is not the New Covenant way.

Nevertheless, having said this, does it mean that you do not need to listen to another brother's word? No. People in the Old Testament period listened solely to their prophets, whereas Christians in our New Testament time not only are to listen to their brethren but are also to add in the guidance of the Holy Spirit. What I said a moment ago does not mean you are not to hear our brother or sister nor search the Scriptures; rather, it calls you not only to do those things but also to add in the guidance of the Holy Spirit concerning those things. Thank God that Moses and Elijah are indeed gone. You do not need anyone to tell you what God's will is, for you can know it in yourself: the Holy Spirit in you will tell you whether you should do this or not do that, whether you should go here and not there, think this or not think that, say this or not say that.

Formerly, I could not understand why Paul insisted on going to Jerusalem (see Acts 21:4, 10-14). A number of people tried to hinder him from going, yet he still went. Why did he insist on going? I now know that Paul had

The Revelation on the Mountain

decided to go in order to preserve the way of the New Covenant. For according to the New Covenant, no one is to be your prophet. True, brothers and sisters may be moved by the Holy Spirit and prophesy concerning you, but some of those brethren back then had no need to tell Paul, since he himself also knew God's will in the matter. Those people were too active in the matter, for they tried to be prophets to Paul. But Paul ignored them and went to Jerusalem as was called for by God. Should Paul have listened to them, what would have happened to the record of the Bible? Instead, Paul went forth, having been willing to sacrifice himself in order to preserve the New Covenant principle and to inform us that today the time of the law and the prophets has passed away.

In our Christian faith there is only the Son of God. We cannot add in law and prophet. Christ the Lord in us causes us to know what we must do or not do. When people ask me for my advice or opinion about matters, I always respond by telling them to ask themselves. Each and every saved person can know God's will in himself or herself. Should our thoughts and emotions be confused, we will not be able to hear the Lord's voice nor the Spirit's leading. But if we are pure in heart, we shall see God and know His mind (see Matthew 5:8). In any case, let us remember that as a Christian we should hear the Lord Jesus and receive revelation from God directly. We must not add in law and prophet. May God lead us in learning a most essential lesson here. First and foremost,

Amazing Grace

let us each receive revelation directly from God himself in Christ by His Holy Spirit, and proceed to know and carry out His will. This, then, is a living covenant which we have, not a dead one.*

---

* Note: Message given on 8 August 1937, probably in the morning.

7: How God Accomplishes His Purpose (1)

"And Jehovah God caused a deep sleep to fall upon the man, and he slept; and he took one of his ribs, and closed up the flesh instead thereof" (Genesis 2:21).

"And Jehovah God made for Adam and for his wife coats of skins, and clothed them" (Genesis 3:21).

"I came to cast fire upon the earth; and what do I desire, if it is already kindled? [*Gr.*: and what is my wish? Would (that) it were already kindled.] But I have a baptism to be baptized with; and how am I straitened [or: pressed in, constricted, cramped] till it be accomplished! (Luke 12:49-50)

"Verily, verily, I say unto you. Except a grain of wheat fall into the earth and die, it abideth by itself alone; but if it die, it beareth much fruit" (John 12:24).

"For even as the body is one and has many members, but all the members of the body, being many, are one body, so also is the Christ" (I Corinthians 12:12 Darby).

"Jesus saith to her, Touch me not; for I am not yet ascended unto the Father; but go unto my brethren, and say to them, I ascend unto my Father and your Father, and my God and your God" (John 20:17).

Gaining the Riches of Christ by Hungering and Thirsting after Christ

A few days ago we together learned of our position in Christ. But for us to obtain the riches in Christ, we must believe. Only those who are hungry and thirsty could believe and hence obtain. Please remember that being hungry and thirsty is not a being dissatisfied. Today there are many who seem not to be satisfied with their lives. They view their present lives as unsatisfactory; yet they do not have a hungry and thirsty heart; therefore, they do not seek after God. Dissatisfaction is negative whereas being hungry and thirsty is positive. Dissatisfaction is that which is related to our present situation, but hungering and thirsting is related to the future. Hence, those who are truly seeking are the hungry and thirsty ones.

I would warn you today that all believers who are merely dissatisfied with life can only know the teaching of the Bible; they are not able to have spiritual experience. If you cannot experience spiritual things, you are the only person to be blamed since the fault is yours. All who are not hungry and thirsty before God can only know the Biblical teaching but cannot obtain the reality in the teaching. I would repeat here that all who do not have a seeking heart after God will simply return to where they were. This is because the truth has no effect on them. May God have mercy on us in causing us to seek after Him and in giving us a living faith to truly live

How God Accomplishes His Purpose (1)

in Christ and receive all the promised riches of our inheritance in Him.

A Brief Review

Today we shall resume looking into the four aspects of Christ's death and resurrection. But before doing so let us briefly review together what we have thus far considered and discussed concerning those aspects of His work. We will recall that we began by considering the first two of four facets pertaining to the death side of those four aspects of Jesus' Calvary work. And the very first facet of the death side which was discussed was the blood of Christ. His blood was shed to redeem us from our sins before God. This facet of Jesus' death is objective in nature and in its effect, in that, due to His dying and shedding His blood, God's life comes to us who believe.

We then considered the second facet of the death side of the four aspects of Christ's death and resurrection; namely, crucifixion, or, to express the matter more inclusively, our crucifixion with Christ in His crucifixion. In our consideration of this facet we noted the fact that man sins because of fallen Adam in us—that is, because of what the Bible has termed "the old man." We saw how the old man in us loves to sin, so our flesh has frequently committed sin. Consequently, for God to save us to the uttermost—that is, save us completely—He needs to rid us of our old man; and according to the

Bible His method is co-crucifixion. To be crucified with Christ is God's way of eliminating the old man. Once the old man is gotten rid of, our new man in Christ is able to live out God's life. The Bible tells us that if we are united with Christ in His death, we for sure will be united with Him in His resurrection (Romans 6:5).

Christ shed His blood and died. Three days later He rose again. This latter fact is proof that His work of redemption has been accomplished. With crucifixion of the old man there is resurrection. And again, such is the objective side. We now have the new man living inside. So we see that blood and crucifixion constitute the negative side of Jesus' work for they deal with the problem of Adam's fall. If Adam had not sinned, there would have been no need for Christ to shed His blood and no need for the old man to have been crucified. But it is due to Adam's sin that Jesus needed to die on the cross. All the foregoing we have already considered together during the previous evenings' discussions on these two facets of the death side to Christ's work. We will now proceed to consider how God accomplishes His purpose.

THE ATONING AND NON-ATONING SIDES OF CHRIST'S DEATH

Before man ever sinned God had already had His purpose and plan in mind. God had wanted man to have His uncreated life so that he might be His son. It was for

How God Accomplishes His Purpose (1)

this reason that He created man, and after he had done so, God placed the Tree of Life before him in the Edenic garden (Genesis 2:8-9). Then, without uttering a word in reference to the Tree of Life He called man to accept His uncreated life (2:16). Man, of course, already had life, but what he had was created life. Being eternal and therefore uncreated, God had desired the created man to possess His uncreated life, too, thus causing human beings to rise above the mere status of man and to be lifted up higher before God. (Let us please note, incidentally, that saying this is not meant in any way to deify man but to signify what God's original purpose for man was and still is: that having God's life, man may henceforth live by God himself.) Yet Adam fell and thus could not realize God's purpose. So God sent His Son to die on the cross for us so that all our sins could be dealt with by the blood and the cross of Jesus.

The Bible, however, further reveals that God's Son has another side to His death which is non-atoning in character. The atoning side of Christ's death has been fairly well known by us, but let us realize that there is a non-atoning side to His death which is also mentioned in the Bible—in fact, it is mentioned a number of times. Today we commit a great error in thinking that the Calvary work of God's Son is totally atoning and nothing more, not realizing that the Bible additionally shows us another side to Jesus' death which is the releasing of God's life from within His flesh so as to cause man also to have God's life.

Genesis 3:21 is a type or symbolic representation of Jesus' death involving the shedding of blood: we are told in this verse that God slew an animal—most likely a lamb (cf. I Peter 1:19)—and used its skins to clothe fallen Adam. But Genesis 2:21-22 gives us a type of another side to Jesus' death. The Bible, in referencing Adam's sleep here, did not mention any shedding of blood but explained that God took a rib from Adam and made Eve.

The slaying of the lamb to make of its skins the needed clothing for Adam points to the atoning side in the death of Jesus: how God through Christ has accomplished the work of redemption and has now clothed us—who were once naked before Him—with the robe of righteousness, even Christ himself. All who are clothed with the skins of the lamb are received by God just as the lamb itself was received. Similarly, all who are in Christ—the Lamb of God (John 1:29)—are accepted by God just as Christ was accepted. Today all the saved ones have come to God through the redemptive work of the Lord Jesus by being clothed with Christ our righteousness (I Corinthians 1:30).

God caused Adam to sleep deeply and made Eve out of his rib. The sleep of Adam is thus a type or prefigurement of the non-atoning side to the death of Christ. From within Christ's flesh God takes out life and gives this life of Christ—which is God's eternal and uncreated life—to man. Out of Christ God takes that with which to build the church.

How God Accomplishes His Purpose (1)

We know from the book of Genesis that God created many animals as well as the man Adam. Those many animals belong to various lower species. In wanting to give Adam a helpmate God did not find such among the animals; so He took a rib from Adam's side and made Eve. Thus, Eve's life is the same as Adam's, not that of a lower species. Nevertheless, man's created life is lower than God's uncreated life in Christ. So now God takes out His life that is in Christ and creates each of us anew so that we may have His life and arrive at His purpose. Such is the way God builds the church with all the saved ones as His materials. The life of the church is therefore the same as God's life in Christ. What life we receive when saved is therefore a much higher life. The life by which we formerly lived was of the flesh and earthly, but now God has given us His life in Christ in order that we might be built up together as the church of God.

Adam's sleep mentioned in Genesis 2:21 does not represent or prefigure the atoning side of Christ's death, for at that moment in the Edemic garden man had not yet sinned. Until sin has occurred there is no need for man's redemption involving the shedding of blood. But an act of sin by man *had* occurred by the time of the death of the lamb told of in Genesis 3:21, and serves as a type of the atoning side in the death of Christ. Garments of skin are only needed once man had sinned. And hence, the slaying of the lamb is representative of the atoning side of Christ's death. It is altogether different from the incident told of in Genesis 2:21. Adam's sleep mentioned there serves as a type of the other side of Christ's death. It was not indicative of a human body's death but was a deep sleep. It can be likened to the physical demise of the saved which for them is actually sleep. Henceforth, we believers in Christ do not die, since death is related to sin. On the other hand, the Lord Jesus declared that whoever is saved shall never die (John 6:47-51, 58). Hence, the so-called death of a Christian should be called sleep for his demise has nothing to do with sin and death.

If we know the Bible, we should be able to differentiate between the atoning and the non-atoning sides of Jesus' death. The latter side is positive for building Christians together as "the bone of His bones and flesh of His flesh" (cf. Genesis 2:23). Christ releases God's life that is within Him in order to create a new man. During the days of His flesh Jesus talked not only about the atoning side of His forthcoming death but also about the non-atoning side—the giving to men God's uncreated life in order to overcome the old creation. To be saved is to have men's sins forgiven, thus rescuing condemned sinners from death. Such is negative in character and all is done by Christ. But He also has the non-atoning side to His death on the cross, which is: to give God's life to us—a life that we never had before. So Jesus' death has its negative side of saving us from death and the positive side of giving us a new life. These two sides are totally different from each other.

How God Accomplishes His Purpose (1)

JESUS CAME TO CAST FIRE ON EARTH

Luke 12:49 and 50 are two verses in the entire New Testament which are most precious yet most difficult to explain. If there be four or five hard-to-explain verses in the entire New Testament, these two verses would have to be counted among them. Here Jesus told people that He came to the earth for a specific reason: to cast fire upon the earth. What is meant by fire here? The fire in view here is not what is related to combustible matter such as firewood. What Jesus had in mind is a fire not of the world; so where would that fire come from? It would come from heaven. Does not the book of Hebrews tell us that God himself is a consuming fire? (12:29) Moreover, in many places of the Bible fire is shown to stand for God's life, for we know that the life of God is righteous and holy as fire.

Hence, we may conclude from the initial words of Jesus recorded in these two verses of Luke 12 that the purpose in Jesus coming to the world was to cast God's fire upon the earth so that people might receive the life of God that was in Him. At the time of His speaking, however, people had yet to receive God's life. So He next said, "What do I desire, what is my wish? Oh, would that it were already kindled." This conveys the thought that He wished people could have God's life that very day, but regrettably they could not. Why was that so? Jesus' next words provide the answer: "I have a baptism [yet] to be baptized with." In other words, the fire could not be kindled because Jesus had not yet been baptized.

Is it not strange that at this point in Luke's Gospel narrative—chapter 12—Jesus is recorded as indicating He had not yet been baptized? But Luke chapter 3 clearly tells us that He was indeed baptized. How do we explain this apparent contradiction? In both Romans 6:3 ff. and Colossians 2:12, we are told that the baptism referenced here by Jesus points to His death and not to His water baptism. So when Jesus said He had not been baptized yet, He meant that He himself was yet to die, and that what His baptismal death on the cross was to accomplish still remained to be realized. What must *this* baptism accomplish, and why? Let us suppose that you are to perform a certain work; what will you do? You will work till its purpose is accomplished. Similarly, Jesus' death is to accomplish God's purpose of giving His uncreated life to people. Since Jesus had yet to die, the fire of God's released life could not be kindled till after His death.

So these two verses in Luke 12 tell us that Jesus came to cast God's fire upon the earth that men might have His life in Christ. Before He died people did not have that life. Only after His death could people receive it. In other words, before Jesus died God's eternal life could not be released and therefore people could not possess it. Why only after His death could people receive God's life? This is explained in what Jesus next declared: "How I am straitened, constricted, and pressed in." Why was He in this condition? The man Jesus had the original life of God

How God Accomplishes His Purpose (1)

within Him, and it was like a seething fire ever seeking to erupt and be spread abroad. That life fills the universe and is normally not limited by time and space. God's life is omnipresent and omnipotent. At any time and in any place there is His life. And here in Jesus' words that life is likened to fire. And an unobstructed fire, we know, quickly spreads and nothing and no one can contain it.

Although Jesus as the Son of God is equal with God, He came to earth to be man. Nevertheless, this boundless divine life was shut up—restricted and compressed—within the flesh of the Son of man. And thus this unbounded life of God was now checked, controlled and restrained by time and space. It could not be everywhere simultaneously. Indeed, if Jesus, the vessel on earth of God's uncreated life, was in Caesarea Philippi, then that life bound up within the flesh of the Son of man could not be in Bethesda at the same moment. This flesh containing the life of God might have been in Galilee yesterday and might today be in Judea, but it could not be in both places concurrently due to Jesus' outer flesh.

Hence Jesus felt very much straitened: His outer flesh confined God's life as a prisoner within the limitation and boundary of time and space. So the Son of God having become the Son of man was not free to express himself unhinderedly as before. How straitened and constricted must be the omnipresent/omnipotent life within Jesus! How could Jesus not have felt straitened all through His years of ministry on earth? Since He had yet to die, He felt extremely cramped and restrained in what He could do. But after His death and resurrection God's life is released. So the other side of Jesus' death was His being relieved of the body's confinement so that the life of God within could at last be released in fullness. And this is the baptism He was to be baptized with.

This facet of Jesus' death causes the Son of man to be freed from the outer prison of His flesh so that He could cast the fire of God's life upon the earth in order that people might receive the eternal uncreated life. Such, then, is the non-atoning side to Jesus' death, which is quite different in character from the blood-and-crucifixion side of His death. The Bible refers to this facet of Jesus' death as relating to the flesh (see, e.g., John 12:24). Due to the limited amount of time left for me to conclude this message, I can only lay a preliminary foundation in helping us to know and understand this other, non-atoning side of Christ's death that causes God's life to be released.

If the Grain of Wheat Falls into the Ground and Dies, It Bears Much Fruit

In considering John 12:24 we shall be touching the mystery of the gospel. "Except a grain of wheat fall into the earth and die, it abideth by itself alone; but if it die, it beareth much fruit." So said the Lord Jesus. This verse of the Bible is most high and extremely important, for it reaches to the very purpose of God. To what, here, did

How God Accomplishes His Purpose (1)

the Lord Jesus liken His death? He likened it to the death of a grain of wheat. We never find the Scriptures employing wheat as a means of representing or portraying the redemption of mankind from sin, since there is no blood involved. On the contrary, Jesus' use of the death of a wheat grain points to the non-atoning side of His death. He is picturing himself here as a grain of wheat. The wheat grain has a shiny outer shell which envelops the life of the wheat inside. In order for the grain's life within to be released the wheat grain must first fall to the ground, be buried therein, and die.

If the outer shell of the wheat grain is not broken or removed, the grain does not pass through death and will never have its inner life released. But if that grain of wheat is buried in the earth, the latter's moisture will work upon the shell and crack it open. After a few days, the released wheat life begins to sprout; and a few months later, it will bear hundreds of new grains.

Jesus likened himself to a grain of wheat with life inside it; and like the wheat grain, unless He dies, He will remain forever by himself: for God has only one begotten Son who alone has God's eternal life within. Now when the living Word who was with God and was God (John 1:1), became flesh on the earth (John 1:14a), and even though He is the Son of God with God's life within Him, nevertheless, that life was surrounded or enclosed by the flesh. As long as this circumstance continued no one could obtain God's life and hence Jesus would be unable to bear any fruit. Originally there is but one grain of wheat—even Jesus—who is the only begotten Son of God. But once His death and resurrection occurs He, like the one fallen grain of wheat, is able to bear much fruit. In other words, that original one grain of wheat now becomes the first of many grains being brought forth or born. Before His death Jesus was God's only begotten Son, but now by the process of death and resurrection He becomes the firstborn Son of God with many other sons of God to follow.

The Church Is the Christ

Let us please note again that before the death of Jesus God had but the one begotten Son. After His resurrection, however, God will now have many children. God's only begotten Son becomes the one firstborn Son. Formerly there had only been the one grain, but after its death that one grain has brought forth many grains. Is there any difference, in the natural world, between the first grain and the latter grains? Please note that when a mustard seed is planted, it bears only mustard. Likewise, when a grain of wheat is planted, it bears only wheat. Similarly, therefore, when Jesus is planted, what will He produce? Of course, He will produce himself.

In Africa there was a particular elderly black sister in the Lord who was most spiritual. Though she was uneducated and could not speak clearly, many went to her for help in spiritual matters. Once a British pastor went to her and asked of her what Christians were. Her answer was that they were bits of Christ. How very true was her reply. No doctor of theology could probably have answered as she had. How very true that every Christian has a bit of Christ in him or her. The many grains of wheat all come from the One Original Grain of Wheat. And thus it can accurately be said that the sum total of those numerous grains is that Original Grain.

All Christians United in Christ Become the Christ

I am amazed by the Bible verse of I Corinthians 12:12. I wonder if you might react in the same way. This verse tells us that though the body has many members, it is one, and so also is the Christ. If you are like me, we all might say to the author of this verse: "Well, brother Paul, you have written incorrectly, for you did not add the word church; you should have said—'so also is Christ and the church'." Yet was Paul really stating the matter incorrectly? Why did he not add "the church"? It is because the church is the Christ, and hence, there was no need for Paul to say Christ and the church.

Let us understand that in the Bible there are two ways of speaking of Christ. Frequently the New Testament's original Greek text speaks of Christ *without* the definite article "the," and such mention of Christ refers to the Lord himself. Sometimes, however, the definite article "the" is placed before the name of Christ; and in such cases, the *corporate* Christ—the church—and not the personal Christ is in view. Unfortunately, in most of our translations of the New Testament this is not indicated. Perhaps only Darby's translation shows the difference. References to Christ and *the* Christ present two different meanings in the Scriptures. The first of these two points to Jesus Christ the individual whereas the second speaks of the church—that is to say, "the Christ" refers not just to the one person Jesus, but to all who are one in Him. In the present context Christ as an individual is not corporate; rather, He is the Head, with all the Christians—the Christ-ones—being joined together as His body. The personal Christ is the Head of the corporate Christ.

Jesus Christ died that He himself might be in us. In each and every saved person there is a bit of Him. Each person has a little, the fact of which is constantly being demonstrated whenever there is the breaking of bread at the Lord's table. The loaf thereon is originally one whole, and thus God calls us to break the bread loaf so as to allow each of us to eat a little. There is only one loaf in the presence of many people. Were we to gather back together all the broken-off pieces to be eaten by the many, there would once again be but the one loaf. In each and every believer there is a little, so all have a little portion of Christ. Such is God's will. Jesus was originally the only begotten Son of God, but after He dies and is resurrected, He himself becomes the Firstborn of God

How God Accomplishes His Purpose (1)

who begets many other sons who are now His brethren (Romans 8:29).

We may wonder in puzzlement how, in the natural world, one grain of wheat can produce many new grains. Though we may not be able to understand how this can occur, nevertheless, we know this becoming many from one is a proven fact in nature. How wise Jesus was in using this circumstance from nature to serve as a metaphor for the non-atoning side of His death. For just as in the natural world one grain of wheat becomes many grains, so also in the spiritual world the one Person, Christ Jesus, can become the many-membered corporate Christ. This, too, is a fact. Jesus is God's "seed" whom God plants in the ground to be buried and die, and the result is that many new seeds—the Christ-ones or Christians—are brought forth in rebirth.

In other words, by death and resurrection the straightened and constricted Son of man was now able to release God's life from within himself to us who believe. And hence, at His resurrection the risen Christ could now rightly say to His disciples, "I ascend unto my Father and your Father" (John 20:17b). Originally God was only *His* Father, but after His resurrection God has also become our Father, for Jesus, heretofore the only begotten Son of God, has now become the Firstborn One among many new sons of the heavenly Father.*

---

* Note: Message given on 8 August 1937, probably in the evening.

8: How God Accomplishes His Purpose (2)

"Wherefore we henceforth know no man after the flesh: even though we have known Christ after the flesh, yet now we know him so no more" (II Corinthians 5:16).

"I will pray the Father, and he shall give you another Comforter, that he may be with you forever, even the Spirit of truth: whom the world cannot receive; for it beholdeth him not, neither knoweth him: ye know him; for he abideth with you, and shall be in you. I will not leave you desolate: I come unto you. Yet a little while, and the world beholdeth me no more; but ye behold me: because I live, ye shall live also. In that day ye shall know that I am in my Father, and ye in me, and I in you" (John 14:16-20).

CHRIST IN THE FLESH VS. CHRIST IN THE HOLY SPIRIT

In the Gospel of John we see that the Lord Jesus himself was in the Holy Spirit as He called us to receive Him. Once Paul knew Christ after the flesh, but now he knew Him no longer in such a way (II Corinthians 5:16). For Jesus is the Living Word that became flesh, being God clothed with flesh (John 1:1, 14a). He came to the world as a man. As it were, the flesh was His garment, He having been clothed with flesh. But after His death and resurrection, Jesus is now clothed with the Holy Spirit. As He formerly was clothed with flesh, so now He is clothed with the Spirit. Before He went through death He had the Holy Spirit in Him, but after His resurrection He is now in the Holy Spirit. When Jesus was on earth, the Holy Spirit in Him was with the disciples; but after He was risen, He now dwells in the believers by the Holy Spirit. Formerly it was the Holy Spirit in Him but now it is Christ through the Holy Spirit. Formerly Jesus was in the flesh but now He is in the Holy Spirit. Formerly Paul knew Christ after the flesh, which means he knew Christ only in the flesh, but henceforth he no longer knew Christ as such. What does this statement of Paul's mean? It means that he thereafter knew Christ as being clothed with the Holy Spirit.

There is a vast difference between Christ clothed with flesh and Christ clothed with the Holy Spirit. As was pointed out last time, when Jesus lived in the flesh He was always limited by time and space. If He happened to be in Galilee He could not be in Bethsaida. While He was by the seashore He could not be inland at the same time. Sometimes His disciples followed Him but at other times they left Him; they were not able to be with Him all the time. Jesus could only be in one place at one time. Were He in Judea and they in Galilee His disciples could not follow Him. Because of His living in the flesh, Jesus became an outside objective Savior. What, then, could people do? Perhaps they could go to Jerusalem thrice a year to worship Him, but upon their leaving that place, they were again separated from Him. At the right location a person could have been with Him; otherwise, that person would have been unable to be with Him. Such, then, was the situation for Jesus while He was in the flesh.

Today, however, the Son of man is no longer in the flesh, having been released from it through death; for in resurrection Jesus took on a spiritual body. By means of His resurrection He became clothed with a different garment, having now been clothed with the Holy Spirit and now living in the Holy Spirit. It was at Bethlehem that the Son of God came into the world for the first time, but He did so being clothed with flesh. After His death and resurrection, however, Jesus put on the Holy Spirit and can thus dwell in us who believe. The Holy Spirit is Christ Jesus. He who formerly lived on earth clothed with flesh had the Holy Spirit in Him, but after His resurrection He is in the Holy Spirit who is non-matter, and can therefore be, and is, omnipresent. And thus Christ in the Holy Spirit is able to live in us, for by simply believing, we can be born again and are able to receive Christ into us.

Can we grasp the significance of all this? When God the Son came to be man, people were unable to receive Him into their spirits. But now that He is in the Holy Spirit, people can readily accept Him to be their life. The coming of the Holy Spirit is therefore most important, for without His coming, Christ would not be in the Spirit, and thus man could never be united to the Lord. Thank God! Today Christ is not just an outside objective Savior but is also the life within us. Thank God that today we are in

Christ and are already united with Him in one Spirit. In realizing this we can see how complete is the salvation of God. He caused His beloved Son to die and to rise again that His Son might live in us and accomplish the purpose which Adam failed to reach.

This, then, is the "another Comforter" (John 14:16a). Why "another"? This word indicates that the Holy Spirit is the second Comforter. There was one already, now here is another. Jesus himself is a Comforter, and the Holy Spirit is also a Comforter. Christ in the Holy Spirit becomes Comforter that we might not be left desolate as orphans (John 14:17c, 18a mgn), but are given strength for the journey ahead as the pilgrim sons of God. Today, each and every believer is able to have Christ dwelling within as the life of God. We not only have our sins forgiven and the old man crucified but we also have God's life living in us. And in the Bible this life is represented to us by the use of the term "flesh" in contrast to the term "blood."

BLOOD IS FOR EXEMPTION FROM DEATH BEFORE GOD, FLESH IS TO POSSESS LIFE IN US

We have already considered together the four facets of the death and resurrection of Christ. First, blood; second, crucifixion—that is, co-death; third, flesh; and fourth, bearing the cross. We have also considered the difference between co-crucifixion and blood. We next are going to discuss the difference between the flesh

How God Accomplishes His Purpose (2)

and the blood. Let us recall from Exodus 12 how God ordered the Israelites to slay a lamb and put its blood on the two side posts and the lintel of their homes. When He passed by and saw the blood, He would pass over all their homes so that they would not die. In the light of this event we can conclude that blood is wholly for God. As that original Passover began, the children of Israel took their staffs and prepared to go on their journey out to the wilderness. The blood had completed their redemption; therefore, the people of God should now run the race that is set before them. Thus, as soon as people get saved they should pursue the kingdom course with their backs towards the world just as the Israelites had turned their backs on Egypt. As soon as the blood is applied, the earthly pilgrim journey of God's people immediately starts.

Yet where came the strength for the Israelites' journey? How did they leave Egypt? Here we can see how God had prepared them—and us, today, for that matter—for this second step. Blood is to redeem God's people of their sins before God. He the righteous God must judge sins, so He requires blood. Blood is therefore exclusively for God. But when a lamb is slain, there is not only blood, there is also flesh that is brought into view. So God instructed the children of Israel to roast the lamb's flesh and eat it so that they would have the strength to go on their journey to Canaan. Hence, blood is for God whereas flesh is for His people. Blood is to be exhibited before God but flesh is for His people to consume. So today blood is to satisfy God's righteous judgment and flesh is to give us believers strength to walk on God's pathway by that flesh being our inward life.

Suppose you ate some meat last night; by the next day it has become your life. In other words, last night's meal of flesh has become you, it having become your inward strength, power and life. In spiritual terms, therefore, we Christians live by eating the flesh of the Lamb of God. We can thus conclude that the blood of the Lamb of God is objective to us in its impact whereas the flesh of the Lamb is subjective in its effect upon us. Jesus' blood is exhibited outwardly to God as the basis for His forgiving us of our sins, while Jesus' flesh is to be consumed inwardly by us, and by so doing we have the strength to make our way along life's journey which lies ahead for each of us.

The problem in today's church lies in the fact that believers depend on the blood of Jesus for the forgiveness of sins but they have not depended on His flesh for providing the strength to walk. God has not given us Christ just to redeem us of our sins; He has given us Christ also to be our very life. In the Bible this truth and reality is represented by the flesh. Yes, the door posts and the lintel had to have the slain lamb's blood applied thereon, but let us not overlook the fact that the children of Israel had also to eat the lamb's roasted flesh—a picture of how it is also necessary for God's people today to receive Jesus the slain Lamb of

How God Accomplishes His Purpose (2)

God into themselves to be their life. All Christians today have their sins forgiven, yet many of them are weak in their Christian walk: they cannot overcome and are unable to press on: Jesus' blood has been applied but His flesh—He himself—has not been eaten, and hence this weakness. In view of this condition in their Christian experience, people should not depend on Christ's blood alone but must also eat His flesh. All who, as it were, take no meat cannot satisfy God's heart. A weak life in a believer in Christ is not God's life.

Two years ago I was in Kaifeng. I asked a group of Christians there what in the Bible is the meaning of Christian life. A sister said, "It means that a believer does not love money, never does wrong, never loses his temper, and never criticizes others. No one who is of the world could do so." Correct, for none can; but God has never asked us believers to exert our own effort to accomplish such a life. For it is not God's will for us to live out man's life; rather, He wants us to live out His life. He never requires us to do what we cannot do, for in and of himself man can only live man's life and do man's work. Instead, God gives His life to us; so that in us there is the life of God that is able to do all which we cannot do. Hence, it all depends on whether we Christians shall allow the life of God within us to be lived out from us.

The problem today lies in many having assurance of their salvation but being weak in their experience. Yes, indeed, they have depended on the blood of Christ, but they have never taken in the flesh of Christ to be their life. They therefore live in the world in as weak a state as do the people of the world.

Such is not God's purpose. He wants man to have His holy, victorious and separated life. God does not want us to be man alone. He puts His life in us that we may do what we cannot do in and of ourselves but can only do by His life in us. The question therefore becomes, Have you eaten Christ's flesh?

DURING BREAKING OF BREAD, FIRST LOAF THEN CUP

Why does the Bible call the Lord's Supper "the breaking of bread" (Acts 2:42; cf. v. 46, 20:7) and not "the drinking of the cup"? For in simply referring to this Christian sacrament as the breaking of bread, the Bible is including the aspect of the drinking of the cup. Indeed, Luke's narrative in Acts 2 is very much in keeping with the words of Jesus who had inaugurated this sacrament which we today call the Lord's Supper or Breaking Bread. For as He was eating His last Passover meal with His disciples, Jesus did and said the following: He "took bread, and blessed, and brake it; and he gave to the disciples, and said, Take, eat; this is my body. And he took a cup, and gave thanks, and gave to them, saying, Drink ye all of it; for this is my blood of the new covenant, which is poured out for many unto the remission of sins" (Matthew 26:26-28 mgn; cf. Mark 14:22-24, Luke 22:19-20). Bread represents the life of Christ whereas the cup stands for the redemption of

How God Accomplishes His Purpose (2)

Christ. The cup was necessary because of Adam's fall. Bread, however, represents the life of the Lord, which is God's life which God wants to be the life of man. His primary purpose is therefore centered on the bread and not on the cup. Though God certainly wants and needs the cup, His central aim is not to be found in the cup; for the latter is only remedial in nature; it is the bread that arrives at God's purpose. That is why the Lord's Supper is also called "the breaking of bread" and not "the drinking of the cup," since the cup represents redemption whereas the bread represents life—even God's life.

The blood or cup is one facet of Christ's death, while the flesh is another important facet of His death. We have already mentioned that this other facet of death is related to the release of God's life. And such release is symbolized in the Bible by the breaking of bread. We are sinners who have our sins washed clean through the Lord's blood. Why, then, during the observance of the Lord's Supper do we not drink the cup first? For in so many words are we not first saved through the effect of what is meant by the drinking of the cup? Yet God in His word instructs us to eat the bread first in celebrating the Lord's Supper together. This is to help us to realize what the purpose of God is, which is for us to accept and take into ourselves the Lord's life as our life. Christ's blood is considered secondary in the Lord's Table observance, for it is remedial in its aim. On the other hand, bread is considered primary in the observance since it represents something higher than blood.

May we come to see clearly God's purpose here. I sense that the greatest difficulty in our Christian walk lies in the emphasis which too many of God's children place upon redemption as over against God's original purpose. But redemption is only remedial in character in redeeming us from sin but does not represent God's original will. For before God created man He had already had His purpose and plan in mind. He was not simply intent on creating man but that after man's creation He in addition had desired man to possess His life. Hence in His spoken words to His disciples the Lord Jesus made sure to speak of the bread first before He mentioned the cup (see again Matthew 26:26-28, Mark 14:22-24, Luke 22:19-20). And the record of Paul's writings has exhibited the same (see, e.g., I Corinthians 11:23-25). Since this is the way taught in the Bible, we ought to observe this very emphasis in our Christian walk. On the one hand, many church leaders nowadays are even unclear on the matter of redemption. They have drifted too far away. On the other hand, it is also wrong for us only to emphasize redemption since the latter itself, though certainly important, is not as important as having Christ as our life.

God's Purpose Is the Flesh

Let us be clear that God's original purpose finds its realization in the flesh because having Christ's flesh is having God's life. We believe we can approach God as

How God Accomplishes His Purpose (2)

soon as we are saved, since we are born of God and now share in His life. Yet to receive glory and reward is dependent upon our allowing God's life to be lived out through us. Romans 3:23 declares all have sinned and come short of the glory of God. What is the glory of God? It is God himself, His dwelling, and His presence; for the God of glory dwells in glory. Since all have sinned and come short of God's glory, none can dwell with Him. Yet in referencing the mystery of the gospel the last clause in Colossians 1:27 declares: "which is Christ in you [that is, in the saints], the hope of glory" (see also v. 26). Sinners cannot approach God but the saints of God, who have Christ in them, can do so, for they have the hope of glory resident within them.

Christ in us is the purpose of God. Hebrews 2:10 tells us that God's original purpose has always been to bring many sons to glory: "it [was fitting for] him [God], for whom are all things, and through whom are all things, in bringing many sons unto glory, to make the author of their salvation perfect through sufferings." What is meant by the two phrases "for whom" and "through whom" in the first part of that same verse? "For whom" means that all things will return to God, and "through whom" signifies that all things come from Him. Thus all things both come from and return to God. What, then, is His purpose? First, God wants many sons; second, He wants these many sons to enter into glory. And all of this is for the sake of "mak[ing] the author [or, captain] of their salvation [Christ] perfect through sufferings" (v. 10c).

And the following passage, verse 11, has these words: "For both he that sanctifieth and they that are sanctified are all of one: for which cause he is not ashamed to call them brethren." Who is "he that sanctifieth"? It is Christ. And who are "they that are sanctified"? These are the Christians. Both the Sanctifier and the sanctified are one. In other words, Christ and the church are one. This word one has reference to God. Christ comes from God, so also is the church from God and therefore receives her life from God. Hence that which becomes a sanctified church through Christ—that which is formed in and by the life of Christ—comes from God. Consequently, Christ is not ashamed to call us His brethren because both He and we come out from God. Accordingly, for Christ to call us brethren is a manifestation of the purpose of God. His eternal purpose is for Christ to have brethren and for God himself to have many sons.

Now we can see clearly before God that His salvation is full and complete; for He causes our sins to be forgiven through Jesus' blood, causes our old man to be crucified with Christ, and causes the resurrected Lord's flesh to be given to us to become our new life. Nevertheless, though all of us believers may have God's life already, for many of us that life has not been lived out; hence, there continue to be defeats and weaknesses. Through death Christ's flesh becomes eatable. By eating His flesh we receive God's life. Whereas the Lord's blood makes us alive once more, it is the Lord's flesh that gives us life. These are two different things. Before God we should die because of our sin; however, by Christ shedding His blood as our substitute we need not die. Originally we had no life but fallen Adam's; but our taking of Christ's flesh gives us God's life. The application of Christ's shed blood has in view a negative purpose, but the giving of His flesh is for a positive purpose. If we exercise living faith, we can enjoy the benefit of all the work of Christ at Calvary. With living faith we can have God's life as our life.

John 6:47-58

In this connection there is a most interesting and relevant statement which Jesus uttered halfway through a lengthy discourse on the Bread of Life that is recorded in John's Gospel chapter 6. And here I would focus our attention on His words to be found in verses 47 to 58. Verse 47 is Jesus' relevant statement, whose truth He underscored with the opening words, "Verily, verily I say unto you"—"he that believeth hath eternal life." So by Jesus declaring that whoever believes has eternal life we come to understand that the one who believes immediately comes into possession of God's eternal life and that he will live forever without death.

Further on in this same John 6 passage we read of Jesus also saying that if anyone eats the bread which comes down out of heaven he will live forever. And His flesh, said Jesus, is this bread from heaven (v. 51c). Whoever eats His flesh, Jesus went on to say, shall have eternal life (v. 54a). The giving of His flesh is for giving people God's life (v. 51c). Let us understand that this word was not meant for sinners. Sinners need to be delivered from death. All who are created by God but have not believed in His Son have only created life, they do not have God's uncreated life. But now the Lord gives the heavenly bread to men to eat in order that they may have God's eternal life. And the bread is Jesus' flesh. We must therefore pay as much attention to Christ's flesh as to His blood. I hope, in fact, that we will not pay more attention to His blood than to His flesh as many of us have previously done. For Jesus himself placed more emphasis on the flesh. Indeed, He told us that His flesh is to be our life (vv. 47-51).

When the Jews heard this, they did not understand and argued among themselves, saying, "How can this man give us his flesh to eat?" (v. 52) So Jesus responded by saying: "Truly, truly, I say to you, Except you eat of the flesh of the Son of man and drink his blood, you have no life in yourselves" (see v. 53). Here we read of the Lord Jesus mentioning flesh before mentioning blood just as was pointed out earlier He would do later when eating His last Passover meal with His disciples and instituted the Lord's Table or Breaking of Bread.

"Since then the children are sharers in flesh and blood, he also himself in like manner partook of the same" (Hebrews 2:14a). In this passage in the original

How God Accomplishes His Purpose (2)

Greek manuscript flesh is again placed before blood by the God-inspired writer of this New Testament book. God pays great attention to making sure that the wording of the Scriptures is always accurate. And here He wants us to see that flesh is what He especially places emphasis upon.

Let us consider again this verse from John 6: "Except ye eat the flesh of the Son of man and drink his blood, ye have not life in yourselves" (v. 53b). Here we notice that flesh and life are closely related. People gain life through eating flesh. Yet without having their sins washed away by the blood first, they are unable to receive life. Unless the problem of sins is solved before God, there is no way to have God's life resident within. In His words here Jesus is heard placing flesh before blood to show us that without eating His flesh we are not able to have God's life. And in mentioning His blood behind that of His flesh, He wants us to know that without the remedial act of redemption through His shed blood, none can obtain His flesh. In the preceding two verses in this lengthy John 6 passage the flesh alone is mentioned. Now, though, both flesh and blood (and in *that* order) are brought into view together for the purpose of showing us that Christ's flesh is of primary importance, with the mention of His blood following secondarily.

Why is it that Christians will be resurrected at the second coming of the Lord Jesus while the unbelieving must wait till the time of the judgment of the great white throne? It is because Christians have in themselves

God's eternal life through Christ. All who have that life may enter into that life at the coming again of the Lord Jesus. As soon as Christians hear God's call, they will arise and enter into His glory. But all who do not have God's life shall enter into death. The believing ones who had been buried in the earth's graves are able to rise up in resurrection and enter into God's life and glory (see John 5:24-25, 28-29). This is because all believers in Christ have had His blood applied and have eaten His flesh and hence, they are able to rise up and be united with God in Christ on that day.

The Lord has shown us that His flesh is eatable. If He says His flesh is eatable, then we can surely eat. As was indicated a few moments ago, we see that in this section of John 6 Jesus had placed flesh before blood; and furthermore, before He brought into view both flesh and blood together, He earlier had once mentioned flesh without even mentioning blood (v. 51c), followed, then, by four successive times in which He mentioned flesh first and blood next (vv. 53b-56). All these serve to indicate to us how much more important is the flesh of Jesus than His blood. Through His shed blood we escape from death, and by eating His flesh we receive God's life. We who have eternal life abide in Him and He in us. Thus are we united to Christ as one.

How God Accomplishes His Purpose (2)

Experience Christ as Life through Living Faith

Many may be in Christ, yet they lack much in the experiencing of Christ. The reason lies in their lack in exercising living faith. For if you have received Christ with living faith, you ought to realize that not only you are in Christ but Christ is also in you to be your life and your all forever. A light bulb must be put in a lamp that is connected to an electric power plant, and thus will it give forth light. Just so, our being in Christ means that Christ's life, power, light, and so forth should naturally flow through us. Yet this experiencing of Christ is so greatly lacking in the lives of many Christians today.

Ordinarily we say that we eat flesh but never say that we eat blood, for blood—a liquid—is to be drunk. However, in several of these Bible verses we have considered, we noticed that the Lord has put aside the matter of drink, thus demonstrating that His intent is to emphasize eating, not drinking. Eating the Lord's flesh is eating the Lord, for flesh represents himself. He who eats His flesh can live forever; otherwise, he will die.

Here, therefore, we behold Christ placing himself before us with the aim of causing us to know that without accepting Him as our life we cannot satisfy God's demand nor reach to God's purpose. Outwardly we may live on earth, yet actually we are as though dead. May God give us grace, open our eyes, and enlighten us, causing us to see not only the blood and our co-death, but also the flesh. All these facets of Jesus' death are different. May God show us mercy that we may see clearly.*

---
* Note: Message given on 9 August 1937.

9: The Victorious Life

"For to me to live is Christ" (Philippians 1:21a).

"I have been crucified with Christ; and it is no longer I that live, but Christ liveth in me: and that life which I now live in the flesh I live in faith, the faith which is in the Son of God, who loved me, and gave himself up for me" (Galatians 2:20).

"When Christ, who is our life, shall be manifested, then shall ye also with him be manifested in glory" (Colossians 3:4).

MANY CHRISTIANS SEEK VICTORY YET FAIL

We have seen how God's purpose is to make Christ our life. Now we will see why God makes Christ our life. The apostle Paul declared that "Christ ... is our life" and that "for me to live is Christ" (Colossians 3:4 and Philippians 1:21a). Unfortunately, we must acknowledge today that we do not know how to let Christ be our life. Instead, we fall and are weak, we glorify ourselves and are critical of others, we are lacking in brotherly love, we are not Christ-like, are unyielding and not lamb-like, we are full of unclean thoughts, are unholy, and have many other sins unconquered. Christ has already died for us and has become our life. But in our daily living we do not have the experience of Christ living out His life in us. On the contrary, we are as before, being no different than the people of the world. As we were prior to our rebirth, so are we now. Regrettably, we have not advanced; and if we look within, all our sins are still there.

Many Christians are like this. They do not know how to let Christ be their life. Strangely, though they seek and pray to God, confess their sins and ask for His grace, hoping to have a holy life and be able to be humble, gentle and loving; yet, after many prayers their hardness remains the same and their temperaments have not been transformed. In spite of continuous prayers God seems not to answer. They wonder what more they should do before God. In view of all this, I would like to advance our discussion a step further by addressing the key question: What does Christ being our life mean and how can we experience it?

Seeking Victory Demands a Thirsty Heart

I have mentioned before that people who are only dissatisfied may not gain anything, that those who also hunger and thirst may obtain. Let us never confuse dissatisfaction with having a hungry heart. Many may not in fact be satisfied with their lives, yet before God they do not have a heart of seeking positively after Him. They have no dealing with God and have not wrestled with Him. Therefore, the dissatisfied may not necessarily be the hungry and thirsty ones. I would strongly affirm that though there may be dissatisfaction, that will not necessarily result in a person having a victorious life.

The Victorious Life

Only those who are also hungry and thirsty will possess such a life. So, commencing from tonight I wish to point out what victorious life is.

Christ is, and is to be, our very life. The seeking ones alone may experience this. Do not expect to casually pick up or establish a victorious life in your experience. There is no such thing. You may indeed pick up related things along the way, but victory is never something to be casually obtained. Victory does not come by chance, for only the hungry and thirsty may possess it. Even if during this conference only three or five people experience it, we shall thank God.

Christ Overcomes for Us

Briefly stated, victorious life is Christ himself. In giving us Christ God not only wishes us to live by Him but also to make Him our life. He is in us believers to *live* for us and not merely to be in us. Christ died for us on the cross, and today He is to live for us from within. Christ within is not for Christ to give us strength to overcome nor to help us to overcome. Rather, it is needful for us to step aside and let Christ within us be our victory.

May I repeat, Christ within is not for Him to give us strength to overcome nor for Him to help us to overcome but is for Him to conquer for us just as He had died on the cross for us. When Christ died for us, we ourselves did not do anything. Likewise, when He lives today for us, we have no need to exert any strength or effort of our own. Today God has given us Christ to be our life by putting Him in us to live for us. Our old man is already dead, so now it is Christ living for us inwardly. This is complete substitution. If it were not substitution it would not be the gospel of glad tidings: no cross, no victory.

Hence today I will not ask God to give me strength to be patient; it will instead be Christ in me who endures for me. True, I am hard, proud, critical, without love, and full of unclean thoughts. But I do not ask God to help me to overcome these issues one by one; no, it is now the Lord Jesus within me who himself becomes my purity, gentleness, and humility. It is a matter of complete substitution. Unless we are clear on the fact of Christ's substitution, there can be no possibility of our being an overcomer. A person may in fact see his fault before God, yet without his being an overcomer. He may even ask God to help him to overcome, but he will never overcome, simply because God never helps people to overcome, for He knows that we will fail. He therefore crucified our old man and gave Christ to us as our life in order that He might live for us from within and be our victory.

Yet many believers ask God to help them to overcome or to give them strength to overcome. But the solution is not there, for we truly are weak beyond any help, our victory being wholly dependent upon Christ living for us from within us. This, then, is the gospel. Such is God's way of salvation and this is victory.

The Victorious Life

SEEING OUR HELPLESSNESS AND ACCEPTING CHRIST FOR VICTORY

During the last two years I have noticed two common symptoms of weakness among many believers: these are short tempers and worry. Many have known that losing their temper is sin, but they do not know worrying is also a sin. Many cannot control their temper. Neither Bible reading nor prayer seems helpful. After eight or ten years things have remained the same in their lives. There is no solution to their plight. God knows we are helpless, so He gives us a way through by taking us out and letting Christ in us be our life by living and overcoming for us. Sadly, many do not know this and thus have no way of victory.

Once I was preaching in England. A friend came to me and told me that his home was close by. He asked me to visit his house. He had a few boys, but his wife and himself were always defeated and not overcoming. When one child cried, they felt uneasy. When a second child also cried, they became angry. When a third child cried, they could not control their tempers any longer. They tried hard to keep their tempers in check, but they could not do so. The father had therefore insisted that I must go to his home and counsel his wife and himself how they could overcome.

So I went that evening. His wife came up to me and said: "Mr. Nee, you know what victory is. Both I and my husband wish to overcome, but three children are too unmanageable for us. In other matters we can overcome but our problem is with our children. We can endure in the church or with our friends, but with regard to our three children we can do nothing." When I heard this, I began to laugh, for I beheld two more people who could be delivered by Christ. Some people are too ethical and their temperaments too good and thus they can never know what victory is. Only the helpless can the Lord save to the uttermost. This was why I was glad for these two parents who I believed could be helped.

I asked the mother why she asked for patience in relation to her difficult children. She replied that her temper was too quick, hence she had been asking God to give her patience in order that she might be able to control her temper. I said to her: "You yourself are helpless. You have been asking God to give you patience, but He has not yet given it to you. Is that correct?" She replied, "Indeed, I have been asking for eight or nine years and God seems not to hear to give me patience." I said to her: "You ask God for patience, but He knows patience is not what you need, so He does not give it to you. Actually, you have no need of patience." She instantly responded: "Mr. Nee, how can you say this? I have never heard such truth. Do you mean to say that I do not need to be patient?" I answered: "Right, for what you need is Christ. God has made it possible for Christ to be in us as our life. He has been made to us wisdom and righteousness and sanctification and redemption, as well as patience—just as the Scriptures have told us (I

Corinthians 1:30). All which God will give us is in Christ. God gives Christ to you for Him to overcome instead of you."

At that moment she realized that there was no relationship between the way of victory and herself. It was not a matter of herself being victorious but it is Christ who overcomes. This is the secret of overcoming which we find in the Bible. It is no longer I but Christ who now lives in me. It is more than living by the power of Christ; it is basically Christ himself who lives in us. I do not live, wrote Paul, it is wholly Christ who lives. Such is the victory for the Christian. This was God's original purpose which He had set for man in the Garden of Eden. It is for Christ to live in man and for man. Christ to be our life has always been God's purpose.

Once I went to a brother's house. His wife told me: "Mr. Nee, I have failed these days. Everything in the house is fine except that these little children of mine are too naughty. If I shut them in the house, they make a terrible mess in the house. If I let them go outside, they fight with other children. They cannot be quiet while in the house and they cause me worry while they are outside. This causes me to cry. I really am at my wits' end. Mr. Nee, what can I do?" I began to laugh, for when man is helpless, God is able to help. So I said to her: "Is victory to be yours or is it to be Christ's? If yours, then three or four children will be too many for you to control your temper about. If the victory is to be Christ's, can these children—no matter how many—cause Him to be helpless? Never! Today you are defeated because you yourself have been trying to take care of this matter of your temper. You acknowledge you have been impatient. Had you been allowing Christ to live for you, you could surely have been patient."

Victorious Life Is Not Change but Exchange

Let me inquire, Do you see that you yourself are helpless, that you can only be defeated, that only Christ is victorious? We in ourselves cannot, but He can. Our problem today lies in the fact that though knowing we cannot, we nonetheless try by ourselves to take care of the challenging situations we face and do not let Christ take care of them for us. Too many believers are ignorant of the way of victory. They simply ask for power. Yet if you have Christ, you have it all. Victory comes through the substitution of Christ, not by man's effort.

Let us please be clear that victory comes not by our being changed; rather, it is Christ overcoming for us. This is because the victorious life is not a matter of change but is one of exchange. It is not my defeat turned to my victory. Yes, I am defeated, but God puts an end to my defeat by means of the cross that instead places the conquering Christ in me. Originally I was defeated, but now God places Christ in me. He substitutes "Christ" for "I," and then I am victorious. The secret of victory lies in the Biblical notion of "exchange." Many incorrectly expect to be changed but they remain in their old Adamic selves. Only by Christ being our substitute can we be victorious.

Two years ago I was ministering God's word in Chefoo. While there I presented this subject of overcoming. I told the brethren that victory does not lie in a "changed life" but in an "exchanged life." Many believers only think in terms of their lives being changed; God, though, views us as so rotten that there is no way for us to be changed. He knows that in us dwells every kind of sin (cf. Romans 7:18a). Let us therefore not imagine that others can be bandits and harlots but we ourselves never can be; on the contrary, we can commit all kinds of sins. If today we have not committed them, it is only due to the mercy of God in keeping us from having been tempted in such a manner. Today God makes use of Jesus' cross having put away our old man and then places Christ in us to overcome for us. Thus, we experience a totally exchanged life, not a changed one.

God's Salvation Lies in Christ Living for Us

Some ten years ago I had a little money in my pocket. I thought how good it would be if I had enough money to buy a watch. At that time I had six dollars, so I used five dollars and eighty cents to buy a watch. That watch was made in a famous watch factory. Now when I bought the watch, the store gave me a guarantee good for two years for any repair. I brought it home. The next morning I noticed that it ran two-and-a-half hours late. Supposedly every watch was to run twenty-four hours per day, but this watch only ran twenty-one hours and a half. So I took it back to the store and told them so. They said they could repair it. After two days I regained possession of the watch. One day later it ran an hour less. So I took it back to the store a second time for repair. After that repair, I took it home again. The next day I discovered the watch timing had not moved at all. So once more I returned it to the store and told them what had happened this time. They again promised to repair it.

After a week the store gave me the watch back supposedly repaired. The next day, however, I discovered this time that it ran three hours too fast! So when I went back to the store, I told them that ever since I had purchased it twenty days ago, during fourteen of those days the watch had remained in the store and only six days in my home. I therefore wondered aloud to the storekeeper whether this watch was theirs or mine?!? I continued by saying that since the store seemed unable to repair it, could they exchange my watch for another one? But they replied that they had no such rule. The guarantee was only for repairing within two years' time.

Hence we can easily recognize from this incident with the watch that to repair and to exchange are two different actions. To repair is to change what has broken down into that which is good, whereas to exchange what is bad or is flawed for what is totally new is an entirely different action. Let us therefore clearly understand that exchange is God's way of complete salvation. Man continually thinks of asking God for power to improve himself or make himself good. But like that watch of mine, fallen man has been so corrupted that he is beyond repair and, again like the faulty watch, the only way to be perfect is for flawed man to be exchanged for the perfect Man—even Christ. God's salvation therefore lies not in helping you to overcome but in letting Christ overcome for you.

Have you understood what Galatians 2:20 means for you? Basically it is no longer you who live: it means that you are not repairable for living out your life: it is no longer you that lives but it is Christ who now lives in you. This is nothing short of total substitution—even the substitution of Christ who henceforth lives in you and for you. This Bible passage does not even say that you overcome by depending on Christ or that you live because of Christ or that you live by the power of Christ. It simply declares that it is no longer you who live. Basically you have nothing to do with overcoming because it is now Christ who lives instead of you.

Victory Is Christ, Patience Is Christ

Someone told me that he always contemplated to overcome and wanted to do so very much; but, he asked me, How can I overcome? I answered him bluntly that if a person like him could overcome, then the whole world could overcome but that I entertained no hope for him to do so. He became angry and asked why he could never overcome. I replied as follows: "You, like everyone else, are utterly corrupted. Yet this is not what I say; it is God who has declared it. And because of such corruption, you are totally helpless. And that is why I frankly told you that no matter how, you will never overcome." He instantly shot back: "But I *want* to overcome!" So I said to him, "Although *you* may want to overcome, you never will." At that point he began to discern that he in and of himself could never overcome. I further said to him: "God is not expecting you to overcome for you are too corrupted. He knows that you could only be defeated. Therefore, God at Calvary set you aside. No one in the world can overcome. There is One alone who can, and He is Jesus Christ. Apart from Him, there is none who is able to overcome." Upon my saying this he now fully understood that victory only belongs to Christ, that victory is Christ.

Once a Christian brother came to me and told me he could not be patient. Yet this was not the first believer to tell me this. In fact, I cannot count how many times I have heard this same word. Can it be that there are so many bad-tempered Christians that one must conclude that all believers easily lose their temper? I asked this brother: "Are you in lack of patience?" He replied: "Yes, and I always pray, asking God to make me more patient. Perhaps my prayer is not earnest enough, because thus far God has not answered my prayer." He continued:

The Victorious Life

"Mr. Nee, am I right in praying this way?" I answered with these words: "No, for God only engages in wholesale and not retail transactions." "What do you mean?" he asked, obviously puzzled. I explained as follows: "When such a person as you lacks patience today, he goes to God and asks for patience. After a few days he has exhausted himself in seeking for it, yet he still goes to God to ask for patience even more. Perhaps a few days later he recognizes himself as also being proud. So he now approaches God to ask for a little humility. A few days more pass and he sees that he additionally is lacking in love and has been critical of others. Once again he petitions God to help him overcome in these additional failings in his Christian life. But God does not conduct himself in such piecemeal manner, and hence his prayers are never answered." God only engages in wholesale business.

To anyone who comes to Him in faith, God will give all of Christ to that person. And this whole Christ in you will be your gentleness, your humility, your patience, love, and so on. God will not give Christ in bits and pieces. All which He gives is in Christ. With the whole Christ in you, you have all you need. Christ in you will live for you in every circumstance of life. No matter how difficult, how great, and how varied are the challenges to overcoming which you may encounter, He is more than their match from one situation to another. What is victory? Victory is nothing less than the whole Christ. And it is Christ in His totality who overcomes for you in every circumstance.

May God open our eyes to see that we by ourselves cannot overcome. We must give up all hope in ourselves and continually maintain a hopeless attitude. There cannot be a single sight of such hope. Victory is not change but exchange. If it is only a matter of seeking for nothing more than a personal change in ourselves, then let me observe that after three or five years you will find that you shall have remained the same. If, however, it is a recognition and an acceptance by faith that our Christian life is an exchanged life, you will experience Christ's victory immediately. It is not an experience which comes gradually since all such experience comes from God. If you are clear on what is the complete salvation of God—namely, that our life in Christ is nothing less than an exchanged life—then victory for you will be instantaneous in every challenging circumstance of your life. But if any part of God's salvation has its basis in yourself, then you shall remain in the same defeatist state in your Christian walk even after thirty or fifty years.

During the past two years hundreds of brothers and sisters in Christ throughout China have crossed over this threshold of a victory in this instantaneous way just as their being saved initially was instantaneous. As we believe, so is victory. Believe and overcome. Prior to two years ago many in China were seeking for victory in their lives, but they were not able to experience anything in the way of victory by themselves. Only when God revealed to them what the exchanged life was did they

The Victorious Life

cross over. If the victorious life be based upon ourselves, the result will be that we shall remain the same even after a hundred years. But if the overcoming life comes from God through Christ, such victorious living is realized at once in every specific life situation. Victory is not man's work; it is a miracle of God's grace.

May God give each of us grace to see that it is no longer you or I but that it is for us to live miraculously from one challenge of life to another. After one particular Christian sister died, people set up a monument to her memory. On it was written, "She did what she herself could not do." The victorious overcoming life which she had lived did not come out from herself, for it became evident that she could do nothing. All things accomplished in her life had come out from Christ, and hence there was no difficulty in her overcoming. Accordingly, she could do what she herself could never do and say what she herself was unable to say. All is of Christ. We in ourselves have no credit share in such victory. Hallelujah! Christ himself is Victor! He lives in us and lives for us. Let us therefore lay aside our selves and let Him live himself out from us. Thus do we overcome.*

---

* Note: Message given on 10 August 1937.

10: The Victorious Way

"A certain ruler asked him, saying, Good teacher, what shall I do to inherit eternal life? And Jesus said unto him, Why callest thou me good? none is good, save one, even God. Thou knowest the commandments, Do not commit adultery, Do not kill, Do not steal, Do not bear false witness, Honor thy father and mother. And he said, All these things have I observed from my youth up. And when Jesus heard it, he said unto him, One thing thou lackest yet: sell all that thou hast, and distribute unto the poor, and thou shalt have treasure in heaven: and come, follow me. But when he heard these things, he became exceeding sorrowful; for he was very rich. And Jesus seeing him said, How hardly shall they that have riches enter into the kingdom of God! For it is easier for a camel to enter in through a needle's eye, than for a rich man to enter into the kingdom of God. And they that heard it said, Then who can be saved? But he said, The things which are impossible with men are possible with God" (Luke 18:18-27).

"He entered and was passing through Jericho. And behold, a man called by name Zacchaeus; and he was a chief publican, and he was rich. And he sought to see Jesus who he was; and could not for the crowd, because he was little of stature. And he ran on before, and climbed up into a sycamore tree to see him: for he was to pass that way. And when Jesus came to the place, he looked up, and said unto him, Zacchaeus, make haste, and come down; for to-day I must abide at thy house. And he made haste, and came down, and received him joyfully. And when they saw it, they all murmured, saying, He is gone into lodge with a man that is a sinner. And Zacchaeus stood, and said unto the Lord, Behold, Lord, the half of my goods I give to the poor; and if I have wrongfully exacted aught of any man, I restore fourfold. And Jesus said unto him, To-day is salvation come to this house, forasmuch as he also is a son of Abraham. For the son of man came to seek and to save that which was lost" (Luke 19:1-10).

"And he hath said unto me, My grace is sufficient for thee: for my power is made perfect in weakness" (II Corinthians 12:9).

Victory Is Christ

During these past few evenings we have come to see how the Lord Jesus gave His flesh to people—that is to say, He gave His life to you and me to be our life. We do not overcome by the help of Christ nor by His giving us strength or adding power to us. The Bible shows us that victory is Christ himself. Victory is Christ in us to live for us and overcome for us. The outcome of all issues of life depends on whether it is you or it is Christ. Ordinarily we think of ourselves as being good. If it is we, then the good-tempered ones can overcome more easily whereas the bad-tempered can barely—if at all—overcome. We do not realize that natural temperament has nothing to do with victory; rather, the issue is Christ. The good-tempered need Christ to be their life just as much as do the bad-tempered. The issue is, does a person have

Christ as his or her life? If so, the believer is able to overcome.

THE WAY OF VICTORY: THROUGH CHRIST, NOT BY SELF

This evening I would like for us to see how we can let Christ live in us and overcome for us. If we consider these two passages in Luke together, we shall be able to discern the way of victory clearly. In both chapters 18 and 19 we read of two contrasting rich men. In chapter 18 the rich man is also a ruler and the rich man in chapter 19 is likewise a public official. In chapter 18 the man is young whereas the man in chapter 19 is older. In chapter 18 we read that the rich young ruler came forth seeking out Jesus; and in chapter 19 we read that the older man, a tax-collector, also came seeking after Jesus. Both of them were interested in the Lord.

The rich young ruler came to the Lord seeking for eternal life, for salvation. He asked the Lord, "Good teacher, what shall I do to inherit eternal life?" We have seen that eternal life is the everlasting uncreated life of God. By what means can we obtain it? The Lord told him, "You know the commandments: do not commit adultery, do not kill, or bear false witness, and honor your father and mother." By these words Jesus was showing him what he must do. But he replied that he had kept all these commandments from his youth. Then the Lord said: There is one thing you lack doing yet: sell everything you have and distribute the resultant funds to the poor, and you shall have treasure in heaven; and come, follow Me.

This evening all who are rich among us may experience their hearts jumping excessively upon hearing this! To sell all and follow the Lord, that is truly impossible. Nothing else in life matters, so to give up my money and all my possessions—that is asking me to give up my life. Let me observe that the problem does not rest on what the rich should do in order to obtain eternal life. In telling this young man not to commit adultery, and so forth, the Lord was not suggesting to him that he must do all these in order to gain eternal life, for we know from Scripture that salvation is by grace and not works. What Jesus wanted him to realize through His words was that he could not keep God's commands. The Lord was not attempting to show him how high the requirements of eternal life were but to show him how far distant he was from eternal life—to reveal to him his weakness, thus causing him to see that he himself had no way of his own by which to save himself.

Unfortunately the young man did not see this. On the contrary, he responded that he had kept all these requirements from his youth. So in pressing the matter further the Lord told him that there was one thing he still lacked doing—that the one thing this rich young man lacked doing was to get rid of all his riches. The Lord is saying here that we each one of us has a lack. You may perhaps think you have patience, humility, love or holiness, and that you have observed them all in a

The Victorious Way

positive way from your youth. Nevertheless, the Lord would say, "There is yet one thing you lack." Everyone's lack is different. Perhaps you are stubborn, boastful, or perhaps talkative. This one thing or that one thing is not universally the same in everyone. Some people lack one particular thing, others lack something else. Judging by our common experience, each person has his or her particular failure. No one person could commit all kinds of sins at the same time. Rather, each one has his or her special sin and is unable to overcome. Whether a Christian is able to overcome in *all* things is to be tested in relation to that one specific sin.

Many are able not to commit adultery and not to steal, but they are unable to give to the poor. Many can honor their fathers and mothers and also not bear false witness, yet they still are in lack of one thing. You may be able to overcome many sins one by one, and thus consider yourself to be an overcomer in the matter of sin. But I would caution you to hesitate in coming to such a conclusion so quickly. Have you truly overcome every sin? Most likely there is still one which you cannot overcome. Everyone has his or her specific sin, a special one in which he or she is definitely defeated. Whether you are victorious or defeated is to be decided by whether you are able or unable to conquer that particular sin which has bothered you throughout your life up to this moment. Normally there will be one or two such sins that have followed you without end. You encounter it from morning till night. Indeed, you have a special relationship to it and it is a sin which you have committed frequently.

The failure with this young ruler was not adultery or stealing. His weakness and failure was his inability to give his all to the poor. What he lacked lay in this one special area of his life. You and I may lack in some other area. We may think we have overcome all, but in fact there is yet one thing we lack doing. As we review the path of the Christian's victory, we usually begin with overcoming many and varied sins through our own effort, then we discover over the course of many sins that there is one special sin. If we can overcome this special sin, we are victorious, but if we cannot overcome it, we are defeated.

Suppose you have never become aware of any one sin that is always bothering you; that is a sure sign that you have yet to overcome. For whoever has never sensed being troubled by a special sin indicates that he has yet to begin experiencing this life of overcoming. It is something he has never considered. Usually people are bothered by some common sins. It is only when they seek after the overcoming life that they discover that though they are able to deal with many other sins, there exists one special sin which they are hopeless in overcoming.

In Shanghai there was a brother who had conquered many of his sins. He had also given his all to the Lord and His work. But he could not control his temper. As he was seeking for a victorious life, he continually beheld this one sin he could not conquer. Indeed, this one particular sin stood in his way to achieving the victorious life. If only he could overcome this sin, he would be victorious; otherwise, he would remain defeated. So this issue of overcoming is centered upon the one single dominating sin in our lives. We all too often think we are able to overcome. Yet if we were truly able, we would have no need for the Lord to overcome for us.

God allows in your life this one particular troublesome temptation to sin in order to see how you will deal with it. You may have kept all the Ten Commandments, but God says to you: "One thing you lack in overcoming." As was the case with the rich young ruler, God wants you to realize you in yourself are unable to be victorious. Yet we usually think we can, that we are able. In that case, God can do nothing for us except to leave that particular troublesome inclination to sin in us to constantly challenge us as to whether or not we can overcome. That rich young ruler heard this challenge from Jesus but rationalized within himself that he could not possibly give away all he possessed to the poor: were he to do so, he inwardly argued, how could he take care of his future? So, he sadly left. He could not overcome. He may have been able to live a moral and ethical life in many other areas but he was helpless to do so when it came to the issue of money and possessions: he loved these things too much.

Luke 19 tells us of another rich man. He, too, like the young ruler, was no ordinary person but was a public official: the chief collector of taxes in the area. He was an older person than the young ruler. In deciding between these two men, who was more likely to have been a money spender—the younger or the older man? More likely, the younger man, since he would not have experienced the world as much as the older man, nor would he have recognized the power of money as much. In fact, at this point in their lives the older man had lived longer and would thus have been more acquainted with the usefulness of money. Hence, in view of all these factors, it would not be inaccurate to observe that most misers have tended to be older people. We can fairly well conclude, therefore, that most likely Zacchaeus would have loved money even more than the rich young ruler of Luke 18.

Zacchaeus wanted to see the Lord; but due to the great multitude surrounding Jesus he was unable to see Him. So he climbed up a tree, hoping to catch a glimpse of Him as He passed by. When the Lord looked up and saw him, He said to him, "Zacchaeus, make haste, and come down; for today I must abide in your house." And so this social outcast made haste and climbed down, and received the Lord joyfully into his home. Those who were there murmured, "Ha! How sinful is this chief tax-collector, yet the Lord is going into his house and lodge there!" Inside, Zacchaeus resolutely stood up and declared: "Behold, Lord, the half of my goods I am going to give to the poor, and if I have wrongfully exacted anything of anyone, I shall restore it fourfold." By doing this, all his property would be gone. Moreover, what Zacchaeus did was what the rich young ruler could not do. Both these two were rich and had positions of authority in their society. Nevertheless, whereas the young ruler thought he could have eternal life but ended up not gaining it, Zacchaeus had humbly considered himself unfit to obtain eternal salvation and nonetheless gained it.

King Saul of old had been a head taller in physical stature than the other people in Israel (I Samuel 10:23), but Zacchaeus was a head shorter than the multitude who followed Jesus. What Saul could not obtain, Zacchaeus did. Where lay the difference between these two? I believe the answer can be found in what the Lord had said to Zacchaeus: "Today salvation has come to this house, forasmuch as he also is a son of Abraham—the man of faith." Salvation comes from Jehovah, and in the day of Zacchaeus God performed a work of salvation for that sinner's house: Zacchaeus was touched in his heart by the Lord, believed in Him, and was thus enabled by God to give up the money he loved. By contrast, the other rich man could not do so because he had been depending upon himself. Zacchaeus was saved by God for he, like others in Jesus' day, had become a true son of Abraham. All who believe God—all who are of faith— are the true children of Abraham (Galatians 3:7). In the one case the rich young ruler had been planning to gain salvation by his own efforts and had therefore asked the Lord what he himself should do to inherit eternal life. In the case of Zacchaeus, however, he did nothing by himself but humbly came to the Lord in the position of a son of Abraham and simply trusted in the salvation of God.

As we have noticed earlier, formerly these two men were similar in several respects. Both were rich, both were public officials, and both came to Jesus. But there the similarity ended, for morally and ethically speaking, the young man was good while Zacchaeus was bad. Natural conditions, though, really do not matter when it comes to the issue of salvation. On the one hand, the young man neither committed adultery nor killed nor stole, yet he ultimately ended up a failure. On the other hand, Zacchaeus was very bad in having defrauded many people, but he ended up a success spiritually. The young man ended up a spiritual failure because he had considered himself able to gain eternal life but found himself unable and departed from Jesus in extreme sorrow, "for he was very rich."

Upon seeing the young ruler leave, the Lord Jesus was moved to say to His disciples: "How hardly shall they that have riches enter into the kingdom of God." It is not impossible, He said in so many words, but it is hard. Jesus further observed: "it is easier for a camel to enter in through a needle's eye, than for a rich man to enter into the kingdom of God." What the Lord meant was that this rich young ruler had absolutely no way to enter the kingdom of God by himself. When the disciples heard these words of the Lord, they worriedly asked: "Then who can be saved?" Each and every one has a little money in the pocket; who, then, can be saved? So the Lord said in response: "The things which are impossible with men are possible with God." In other words, man cannot, but God can. The rich young ruler could not enter the kingdom because he was depending on himself, whereas Zacchaeus could do so because he believed and trusted the Lord. The one was unable to be saved and went away sorrowfully, but the other joyfully received the Lord and His salvation.

With Man, Impossible; with God, All Possible

Luke 18 shows us what is impossible with man, but Luke 19 shows us that with God all things are possible. Things are impossible with man if such depend for their realization on him. Yet if God is permitted to work in man, He is well able to deliver man. Having living faith in God, man will be able to do what he could not do before. All in the world love money, even children learn to love money. When the Chinese began to learn English, the very first word they wanted to learn was the word for money! Moreover, in the process of creating one's will, a person is actually writing about money. Everybody loves mammon, but God and mammon are opposed to each other. If you are not serving God, declares the Scriptures, then you are serving mammon (Matthew 6:24). In fact, the influence of money is so great that it stands in opposition to God. Here in Luke 18 and 19 the Lord is showing us that if God can deliver us from what we love best, He can also save us from all other sins. With man, of course, that is impossible; with God, however, all is possible.

Let us notice again in Luke chapter 18 that after the young ruler heard the Lord's words that he should sell all his possessions and distribute the proceeds to the poor, he departed in extreme sorrow for he felt the Lord's words were impossible for him to carry out. Indeed, it *was* impossible for *him* to do so. And had his subsequent heart attitude been right, he would have gained the eternal life he so earnestly sought. At this moment, however, this rich young man committed a serious error. For what he did wrong was that upon recognizing his weakness and realizing the impossibility of his being himself able to implement Jesus' words, he went away from the Lord (Mark 10:22), he incorrectly assuming that God also could not. It is right for man to discern and acknowledge his personal limitation, but to consider his situation as totally hopeless and beyond even God's ability to overcome is grossly wrong and a great error.

In Luke chapter 19, though, we find that what is impossible with man is altogether possible with God if only He is allowed to work in us. The way of victory lies in seeing that by oneself it is impossible to overcome, but with God such is possible. God can make us victorious through Christ. If we look to ourselves for overcoming power, we cannot be victorious: we can only be defeated. Yes, we must see and acknowledge the impossibility of our overcoming in and of ourselves; but we must also see that God has given Christ to us to overcome rather than trying to depend upon ourselves. The issue for us need not end, as was the case with the rich young ruler, with man's "impossibility." We cannot, that is very true; yet through Christ, whom God has placed in us, all things are possible.

The Terrifying Bad-Tempered Believer

As I speak I am reminded of one person in particular about whom I believe that if *he* were able to overcome his life-dominating sin, then all other people in the world could also be victorious in overcoming in their lives. Last year in Shanghai a Christian brother and friend of mine who served in a missionary society came to see me. He told me about another person who had been sent by an American foreign mission organization to serve as a teacher in my missionary friend's mission school in Shanghai. This teacher had been there now for some five or six years but was in bad relationship with all his colleagues and students in the school. This had come about due to his very bad temper. All in the school felt helpless, with even those in the mission society believing the situation was hopeless and thinking of calling him back. In fact, the mission school was planning to send him back to the United States in August. So this Western missionary friend of mine came to ask me if I had time to talk with this person. I asked why he had not brought him along that day. His answer was that it would have been quite a task to bring him since he believed this man must be demon-possessed; otherwise, this brother added, how could he be like that?

I thought this word appeared to be excessive, yet I sensed that he could not be too much off the mark. I actually was somewhat surprised, so I asked this brother for more details. He said to me: "This man is truly strange. He never laughs. Every time he meets people, he gives them an unpleasant face. He is angry from morning till evening. Should a person have done or said anything wrong, he would immediately deal severely and most angrily with him. As a matter of fact, everybody is afraid of him. When people see him coming, they immediately try to avoid him. It has been like this now for almost six years. No one in the school can work with him. Servants in the house where he resides have had to be changed every two days. He cannot maintain a good relationship inside the home and quarrels with rickshaw coolies outside. In fact, wherever he goes, he quarrels. It seems as though he has always to be quarreling as his way of spending his days. From my birth till now, during these fifty some odd years on earth, I have never encountered such a bad-tempered person as he. I have been in England, in the United States, and in China, but wherever I have gone, I have never met such a person like him. I am afraid he is demon-possessed. Hence, I am truly disappointed in him. We are therefore thinking of

The Victorious Way

sending him back to the States in August. Mr. Nee, you are a person who truly knows the truth of the way of victory; do you think you can help this man? Before his return I was thinking to invite you to go see him to learn whether or not he is truly demon-possessed, and if so, that you try to cast the demon out."

Upon hearing all this, I was glad, because here again was a person with a humanly impossible situation in his walk with the Lord. When it is impossible with man, it is possible with God. God specializes in hopeless cases. So I promised to go see him. This missionary friend told me, however, that I could not go to his home, for it was certain that he would refuse to see me. He explained that I could only go to another's house, and at the same time, he added, they would bring him there so that I could meet him. So this was our plan.

After two days I went to a certain house as arranged, and that person came. After those who brought him introduced me to him, they all left. As I initially observed him, I was truly frightened, for I had never seen such a person like him. It seemed that every part of his face—whether his eyes, nose, mouth, lips, or other parts, whatever that part was—all seemed to have been specially made for exhibiting bad temper! All his facial features expressed bad temper. I now realized that what my missionary friend had told me was all true. It truly appeared to me that he could hardly laugh at all, for it seemed to me, as I looked at him, that there was no place on his face for laughter. He had developed such alarming facial features through his many years that I had never seen such a person before nor would I see such ever afterwards. Indeed, I was terrified upon seeing him for the first time. In fact, I feared that he was truly demon-possessed after all.

Nevertheless, when he saw me, he began to cry profusely and his tears kept falling down. He exclaimed to me: "They do not want me anymore!" As he wept, his face became so ugly as though he was beginning to lose his temper. At that very moment I became so frightened that I would rather have sat in a tomb for three years than to have been required to sit before him for three minutes. How frightful it would be, I thought, if he should indeed lose his temper!

I asked him, "How do you view yourself?" He explained to me: "I often buy things for others, I preach the gospel, I pray for people. When people are sick, I pray for them and they get well. Except that my temper is a little bad." "Is it just a *little* bad?" I inquired. "To tell you the truth, it is just too bad!" he replied. I further inquired, "Have you been like this from your childhood or is it only recently that you have been like this?" (The reason I asked this was to learn whether this terrible behavior of his was natural or a result of being demon-possessed). He told me: "If I remember correctly, I could beat my father when I was only seven years old. Whenever my temper flared up, I would wildly throw things here and there. It has been like this till now. I am truly helpless. It cannot glorify God and yet I continue to

The Victorious Way

sin. I feel I am the most pitiful person in the world for no one will nod at me or speak to me. The whole world has deserted me, all avoiding me as being the worst person in the whole world."

As he said these things, he again wept. I, however, began to exhibit laughter. So He said, "Please do not laugh at my bad temper." I responded by saying: "I am not laughing at your badness, I am laughing with great joy in the Lord. And the reason is that I am glad that you are helpless, but God is able." He said, "Perhaps you have never seen my bad temper, you thinking that I am still able to be helped." As he said this, it seemed as though he was on the verge of showing me his bad temper. His face was really terrifying.

In response I said to him: "There is no difficulty to solve a problem like yours. It is not hard for you to overcome." He countered with these words: "How can you say this? I have been here praying for these many years, even fasting to this very day. But I am helpless. How can you possibly see any hope for me?" I replied: "You can overcome instantaneously. It is not a matter of whether *you* can or cannot; rather, it is a matter of whether God can. Can you say that because you are so bad God cannot save you? You yourself cannot, but God can. For victory does not and cannot come from you, it can only come through Christ in you. He overcomes for you. Should victory be expected to come from the believer, then it could legitimately be said that those with better tempers could easily overcome whereas the truly bad-tempered could never overcome. The reality of overcoming has nothing to do with good or bad temper. It cannot and does not depend on you yourself; it is wholly dependent upon Christ. It is entirely a matter of Christ in you overcoming for you; for the source of victory resides with Him, not with you."

"Do you really think I can overcome?" he inquired. I answered as follows: "You cannot overcome, you in yourself have no way to overcome. Do you acknowledge this? Even so, though you cannot, Christ can. The solution to your problem lies not in you only seeing 'your cannot' but that also, through seeing 'your cannot,' you come to see that Christ can." To which he responded with this question: "Then what should I do for me not to lose my temper?" I replied as follows: "You are to do nothing; you have already been doing too much all these years and yet you remain the same, unable to overcome. You need to step aside and let Christ do the overcoming. Let Christ who is in you do it for you. Do not look at yourself, look only at the Christ of God. He alone will enable you to overcome."

Then both of us knelt down to pray, I asking him to pray, confessing all his failures before God. So he prayed the following prayer: "I honestly confess that I am totally corrupt. I have no hope in myself. I am helpless. Hereafter, I will not trust in myself anymore. I cannot overcome. O God, You overcome for me. I am forever helpless. From now on, I give up myself. O God, You be responsible."

The Victorious Way

Thus did he honestly pray. When he got up, it was already time for lunch. He asked me again, "What should I do after I go home?" "Do nothing," I replied. "Right, I already forgot. I am to do nothing." Then he laughed. This was perhaps his very first laugh; indeed, I could tell that it was quite unnatural for him to do so. After a few steps he turned and asked again, "Truly, I am to do nothing?" I answered, "Truly, do not do anything. When Satan tempts *you* to try being patient, you must simply say: 'I cannot be patient, but Christ, You be patience in me!'" In response he agreed: "Yes, yes," and he continued by saying: "Now I am to do nothing. If I am to be delivered from my temper, it is God, not I, who does it." He even said this to himself as he walked away.

I was a little concerned whether he had the living faith and whether he would truly lay himself aside. After a few days, therefore, I telephoned to inquire. A person answered me on the phone and explained what had happened: "It is strange, truly strange! The entire school has never experienced such peace. Never in these six years have we seen him so quiet, not a sound is heard. God has manifested His miracle and power in his life."

Today I want to say to us all that if this man can overcome, anybody can. After a few days more, the formerly bad-tempered brother came to our meeting. He was able to laugh. Later, all his colleagues and students testified for him in positive terms. Originally the school was intent on sending him back to the States, but now he had truly changed and hence he was never sent back.

Do Not Accept Satan's Temptation

Thank God that though with man overcoming is impossible, with God all things are possible. Victory comes not from ourselves but comes from Christ! You may not be in as extreme a situation as was that bad-tempered missionary teacher; nevertheless, you must look to Christ and not to yourself for victory over sin and self. If you should look to yourself, you will surely fail. When Satan tempts you, he is not tempting you to commit sin; instead, he is tempting you to try to be good. But in our old man there is nothing good. On the contrary, he only knows how to sin, and apart from death there is no use in him. God calls us to acknowledge that we have died together with Christ, for this is His outlook towards the old man. The old man is only worthy of death. God's attitude towards the old man is simply and only death. The old man deserves nothing but death.

Our error is that in realizing our weakness in a given issue of our life we then ask the Lord to give us strength that we may resist; so that when temptation comes, we by our old man try our best to resist. For example, when Satan tempts us to lose our temper, we try our best to be patient. Yet we do not realize that when we make a move from ourselves to resist, we ourselves come forth, and that is the trouble.

It is very strange that when Satan tempts you, his purpose is not for you to resist but to cause you—that is, your old man—to come forth. Once you come forth, you

The Victorious Way

sin. What Satan is afraid of is that you do not come forth. If you take Satan as your object, you are defeated. Therefore, if temptation comes, do not make a move out from yourself, for you are unable to resist. And as you desist from moving, Satan will leave. You may wonder why temptation goes away. The issue is not you, but Christ in you had overcome.

One day while I was in Chefoo a foreign lady came to see me. She, too, had a problem with bad temper. It seems as though bad temper is a common sin among Christians. She told me how she would lose her temper when her children were quarreling, for she had no way to be patient. I jokingly told her that since she had no patience, she should not try to be patient. She replied that if with great effort she was unable to be patient, what would happen if she made no effort to be patient! I said in reply: "Because you try to be patient, your temper flares up. If you did not try to be patient, you would be all right. Your trying to be patient spoils patience. Since you are not able to be patient, why even try?"

Is God able to be patient enough? With man it is impossible, but with God all things are possible. We need to know and acknowledge that we ourselves cannot do what is required, and at the same time also acknowledge that God is able. Usually we do know we are unable, and yet we still try to do what is called for in a given situation. Consequently, God can do nothing but let us try to do what we cannot accomplish. Victory does not depend on can or cannot, nor does it depend on just knowing and acknowledging that we are unable. Man cannot, he must not think he can, nor should he try to do. Since he cannot, then he should simply let go and let God. Man must not change his self-acknowledged "I cannot" to "I still can"; for by his not doing so, then God will be given the opportunity to show forth His "can do" ability in our lives.

Victory Is a Miracle

Victory is actually a miracle: it is God performing a miracle in our lives. And the secret of such victory lies in facing up to the fact that we cannot and then acknowledging that God himself can and thus allow Him to work in us. Since we *are* unable, let us not try to *be* able or change "unable" to "able." Let us let go, for it all depends on God. It is a total substitution. Just as we are saved by faith at the beginning of our walk with the Lord, so now we only need to continue to believe. When I first got saved, I did not know what overcoming was. Later on, God opened my eyes to see that I was not able, that only God through Christ in us was able. Henceforth, I have walked in living faith towards God and He has brought me through.

May God open our eyes in causing us to see the way of His complete salvation: that we truly must set ourselves aside, accept by faith God's every word, so that His word might be experienced continually in our lives. May God bless His word.*

---

* Note: This message was given on 11 August 1937.

OTHER TITLES AVAILABLE
From Christian Fellowship Publishers

By Watchman Nee

<u>The Basic Lesson Series</u>
Vol. 1 - A Living Sacrifice
Vol. 2 - The Good Confession
Vol. 3 - Assembling Together
Vol. 4 - Not I, But Christ
Vol. 5 - Do All to the Glory of God
Vol. 6 - Love One Another

Aids to "Revelation"
Amazing Grace
Back to the Cross
A Balanced Christian Life
The Better Covenant
The Body of Christ: A Reality
The Character of God's Workman
Christ the Sum of All Spiritual Things
The Church and the Work – 3 Vols
"Come, Lord Jesus"
The Communion of the Holy Spirit
The Finest of the Wheat – Vol. 1
The Finest of the Wheat – Vol. 2
From Faith to Faith
From Glory to Glory
Full of Grace and Truth – Vol. 1
Full of Grace and Truth – Vol. 2
Gleanings in the Fields of Boaz
The Glory of His Life
God's Plan and the Overcomers
God's Work
Gospel Dialogue
Grace for Grace
Heart to Heart Talks
Interpreting Matthew

Journeying towards the Spiritual
The King and the Kingdom of Heaven
The Latent Power of the Soul
Let Us Pray
The Life That Wins
The Lord My Portion
The Messenger of the Cross
The Ministry of God's Word
My Spiritual Journey
The Mystery of Creation
Powerful According to God
Practical Issues of This Life
The Prayer Ministry of the Church
The Release of the Spirit
Revive Thy Work
The Salvation of the Soul
The Secret of Christian Living
Serve in Spirit
The Spirit of Judgment
The Spirit of the Gospel
The Spirit of Wisdom and Revelation
Spiritual Authority
Spiritual Discernment
Spiritual Exercise
Spiritual Knowledge
The Spiritual Man
Spiritual Reality or Obsession
Take Heed
The Testimony of God
Whom Shall I Send?
The Word of the Cross
Worship God
Ye Search the Scriptures

ORDER FROM: 11515 Allecingie Parkway Richmond, VA 23235
www.c-f-p.com

OTHER TITLES AVAILABLE
From Christian Fellowship Publishers

By Stephen Kaung

<u>The "God Has Spoken" Series</u>
Seeing Christ in the Old Testament, Part One
Seeing Christ in the Old Testament, Part Two
Seeing Christ in the New Testament

Discipled to Christ
The Gymnasium of Christ
In the Footsteps of Christ
The Songs of Degrees – *Meditations on Fifteen Psalms*
The Splendor of His Ways – *Seeing the Lord's End in Job*
New Covenant Living & Ministry

ORDER FROM: 11515 Allecingie Parkway Richmond, VA 23235
www.c-f-p.com